ETHNICITIES

PLAYS FROM THE NEW WEST

ETHNICITIES

PLAYS FROM THE NEW WEST

HOUSE OF SACRED COWS

PADMA VISWANATHAN

MOM, DAD, I'M LIVING WITH A WHITE GIRL

MARTY CHAN

ELEPHANT WAKE

JONATHAN CHRISTENSON / JOEY TREMBLAY

EDITED BY ANNE NOTHOF

PRAIRIE PLAY SERIES: 16 / SERIES EDITOR, DIANE BESSAI

NEWEST PRESS
EDMONTON

Canadian Cataloguing in Publication Data
Ethnicities

(Prairie play series ; 16)
Contents: House of sacred cows / Padma Viswanathan — Mom, Dad, I'm living with a white girl / Marty Chan — Elephant wake / Jonathan Christenson & Joey Tremblay.
ISBN 1-896300-03-0

1. Canadian drama (English)—20th century.* 2. Ethnicity—Canada—Drama. I. Nothof, Anne. II. Viswanathan, Padma, 1968- House of sacred cows. III. Chan, Marty. Mom, Dad, I'm living with a white girl. IV. Christenson, Jonathan, 1964- Elephant wake. V. Series.
PS8315.5.P73E83 1999   C812'.5408'0355   C99-910239-7
PR9196.6.E83 1999

Editor for the Press: Anne Nothof
Cover design: Val Speidel Design
Interior design: Brenda Burgess
Cover photographs: Ed Ellis and Ian Jackson

NeWest Press acknowledges the support of the Canada Council for the Arts for our publishing program. We also acknowledge the financial support of the Government of Canada through the Book Publishing Industry Development Program (BPIDP) for our publishing activities.

The Canada Council for the Arts | Le Conseil des Arts du Canada | Canadian Heritage / Patrimoine canadien | Canada

Cover and interior photographs have been reproduced with the kind permission of the photographers.

Damon D'Oliveira as Anand and Brian Linds as Orwell in the Northern Light Theatre production of *House of Sacred Cows*. (Ellis Brothers Photography)

Patrick Gallagher as Kim Gee, Caroline Livingstone as Sally Davis, and Jared Matsunaga-Turnbull as Mark Gee in the Theatre Network production of *Mom, Dad, I'm Living with a White Girl*. (Ian Jackson)

Joey Tremblay as Jean Claude in the Catalyst Theatre production of *Elephant Wake*. (Ellis Brothers Photography)

Printed and bound in Canada

NeWest Publishers Limited
Suite 201, 8540-109 Street, Edmonton, Alberta T6G 1E6

CONTENTS

INTRODUCTION:

FRAGMENTING THE MOSAIC

T he comfortable myth of the "cultural mosaic" is an imaginative
construct which reifies the Canadian self-concept of tolerance,
freedom, and diversity. It configures social harmony as a pleas-
ing aesthetic pattern: the juxtaposition of many, small, brightly-
coloured pieces to make "a work of art." It should be remembered,
however, that the mosaics which constituted the iconography of the
Roman and Byzantine Empires reaffirmed religious and epistemologi-
cal beliefs. A mosaic imagined as a social metaphor also assumes that
each piece in the society has a preferred place, in keeping with the
grand design. Whether the piece fits or not determines the nature of
its reception. On the other hand, such a construction of a "national
character" resists the notion of assimilation—as configured in the
American social myth of the "melting pot." In Canada, diversity and
distinctiveness are tolerated, even encouraged, when they are perceived as indicators of a rich and colourful social fabric, without sub-
versive political indications. As Sally, the "white" girlfriend of the
Chinese-Canadian protagonist in Marty Chan's play, comments, "we
will sanitize his quaint customs and add them to our multicultural
mosaic. . . . We'll take egg rolls and fortune cookies. Maybe a dragon
dance. But not communism unless it comes with Mao jackets." From
the perspective of the immigrants, the cultural mosaic may not be
quite so benign a metaphor. They may resist the way in which they
are placed in the grand design—usually on the edges. They may also

fear that their traditions and history may be lost, that their children will become so integrated with the pattern that they will forget their connections with their heritage and their language. Ironically, this cultural fear also pertains to the descendants of those who are historically perceived as "indigenous" or as "founders"—the First Nations, the Métis, the French. They experience marginalization in the country of their ancestors. As the sole survivor of a once thriving francophone village in Saskatchewan, Jean Claude, the protagonist of *Elephant Wake*, imaginatively reconstitutes the fragments of his French-Canadian pioneer heritage in defiance of insouciant anglophone dominance.

In the English-Canadian construction of a cultural mosaic, those who are perceived as not constituting the post-colonial matrix of an "Anglo" society are designated to be "ethnic"—an exotic "other" differentiated by race, language, culture. The term "ethnicity" may evoke colourful images of folk dances, traditional costumes, an accented English, but it also has racist underpinnings. The Greek root word for "ethnicity," *ethnikos*, means "heathen"—one who is unenlightened, lacking in culture or moral principles. Any group which departs from the "norm" of anglophone, European culture is typically cast as a foreign element, which may be threatening or enriching, until fully integrated with the whole. However, when the "ethnic" element confronts these assumptions, and resists placement in the social mosaic, then there is also the possibility for a dislocation of the Anglo hegemony.

The title of this anthology, *Ethnicities*, on the one hand signals that the three plays constitute a departure from the "norm" of western Canadian plays—rural, realistic, white, Anglo; on the other hand, the title suggests the presence of a complex, diverse, and imaginative theatre. In each play, there is a resistance to the prevalent social design, or a conflict which replays the cultural collision within the protagonist. The "mosaic" may be fractured or reconfigured.

In her essay, "Writing the Immigrant Self: Disguise and Damnation" (*In Visible Ink: crypto-frictions*, NeWest Press, 1991), Aritha van Herk suggests that those who attempt to write the immigrant experience create an imagined self in the form of a story which effects a necessary transformation for survival: "the writer writing the immigrant fiction usually writes not from the safe distance of a given exterior (the objective eye/this *I*) but from within the implied fiction—a subjective and hence implicatory position where all the eyes of Argus would not be enough to see the story clearly" (177). The overt story almost inevitably is doubled by a covert story. The prototypical immigrant dream, as recounted in the overt stories of many immigrant "fictions," shows how an arduous journey to the land of opportunity, diligent hard work, and compliance are rewarded by "success" in terms of property and a dynasty. The three plays in this anthology foreground the covert story—the ways in which the "ethnic" imagination may reinstate and reaffirm an old world in the new.

House of Sacred Cows, Mom, Dad, I'm Living with a White Girl, and *Elephant Wake* have in common a Western Canadian location, but the settings are as diverse as can be imagined—a co-op house in Edmonton, an acupuncture clinic in Vancouver, a small French community in Saskatchewan. The protagonists are similarly diverse: a Tamil Indian Masters student, a young Chinese-Canadian mechanic, a French-Canadian prairie existentialist. What they have in common is their resistance to the hegemony of Anglo society: this resistance may be active, passive, or even unrealized until a decision has to be made about where their loyalties and beliefs reside.

In Padma Viswanathan's *House of Sacred Cows,* the "ethnicity" is performed through the brief occupation by an Indian student of a room in a co-op in a Western-Canadian city. The co-op functions as a microcosm for Canadian society, with its social and political struggles, its shared ideals and ongoing fractiousness, its conflicts between the "haves" and the "have-nots." January, the daughter of the founder of the co-op, attempts to reinstate the original ideals of democracy and equality, and learns that even democracy cannot be imposed. Leaf, the single mother who has absorbed the rhetoric of self-realization, is wholly preoccupied with her own needs. Orwell, like his namesake, is concerned with social equality, but finds himself working for a Tory government and absorbing some of its business tenets. He is also unclear about his sexual orientation. The twin brothers, Guy and Gui, both of whom claim to be the true father of Leaf's child, manifest opposing philosophies of pacifism and aggression. In this retreat from the "radical right" of Alberta politics, there seems little possibility of establishing a utopian society, since each occupant has a different way of seeing things, and a resistance to abiding by the rules of others.

This fraught society is even further complicated by the arrival of a "foreign element," accompanied by the ghosts of his dead parents. They refuse to abandon him to the idiosyncrasies of Canadian society, and try to induce him to return to his family obligations and traditions in India. That he is very much aware of the extent to which he as an individual is informed by his culture and religion is evident in the stories he tells from the *Mahabharata*, a Hindu epic which recounts the conflict between five brothers and their one hundred cousins. The "sacred cows" in this house are shown to be both negative and positive values; the trick is to differentiate them. For the Canadian residents, Anand brings with him the wisdom of the East. They do not question the presence of his parents, who constitute the "otherness" of his Indian origins, both literally and metaphorically. In a sense, Anand is reconfiguring the mosaic of the co-op through his stories and his advice, even though he seems almost incapable of decisive action himself. The East infiltrates the West, and at the end of the play, he is joined by January when he returns to India for his uncle's funeral and his sister's marriage. The emigration can go both ways.

In Marty Chan's *Mom, Dad, I'm Living with a White Girl*, the spy-thriller film which runs as an imaginative counterpoint to the "actual" events of the play shows the nefarious means by which the East will try to take over the West, how the threat of the "Yellow Peril" will be enacted. The play speaks not only to the history of Chinese immigration, but to current phobias and racism, which become targets for its satirical humour. Marty Chan turns the mirror on his audience, so that it will see clearly the racist assumptions inherent in "ethnic" jokes. "Politically correct" responses are also exposed as patronizing and demeaning—as an attempt to speak for other people, another kind of "appropriation of voice." In the debate between the "White Girl" and her Chinese boyfriend in the play, the controversial issue of "ownership" is raised, replicating the playwright's own experience of being charged with discrimination against his own people. According to the "liberal" girlfriend, Sally, "ethnic" writers should "leave the stupid stereotypes behind. It's just going to give racists permission to use these awful jokes themselves." Mark's response is that racists have never needed "permission to be assholes," and he would prefer to have everything out in the open. In *Mom, Dad, I'm Living with a White Girl*, the caricatures of Asian villains which have informed Western popular culture are the means by which the young Chinese protagonist attempts to establish his autonomy. The traditional values of his parents are parodied as a sinister plot. However, Marty Chan's "hero" wields a double-edged *shuriken* (Chinese throwing star): he resists total adherence to his parents' expectations, but also resists the assimilative pressures of Canadian society. In this play, "Canadianness" is also satirized for entrenched and unacknowledged racism, but also for apathy and ignorance. The protagonist is placed between the two cultures, attracted to the freedom promised by the "white" society, but finally also aware that he cannot disassociate himself from his own distinctive heritage. There is no final celebratory marriage in this comedy: the *komos* is subverted.

Elephant Wake is a lament for the dying French culture in the prairies, subsumed by an anglophone hegemony. The protagonist, Jean Claude, is the last member of a once extensive Catholic family to remain in the large ancestral home. Like the Chinese elephants which he reconstructs in papier-mâché, his "race" is almost extinct. But he insists on survival, constructing for himself, as he has learned from his grandmother, a zoo full of creatures—an imaginative world that he can safely inhabit. He cleans up the indicators of abandonment, and performs his own celebration of faith and hope. Ironically, Jean Claude is an "immigrant" in his own land—an outsider in terms of the dominant English culture, much like his friend, the Métis 'tit Loup. Like 'tit Loup (little wolf), he is an endangered species. But he refuses to admit defeat, and constructs from the "bones" of what remains a larger-than-life testimonial to survival, which can be seen for miles across the prairies. As his nicknames suggest, he can be viewed by others as a weed (chou-gras), growing in a ditch, or as a saviour (J.C.). And even in the ditch he can see the stars.

If these three plays can be construed as "Western Canadian" or even "Canadian," it would be because of the ambivalence of the endings. There are no "conclusions," no "happy-ever-afters." There may be a kind of accommodation, or an indication of an ongoing struggle against the prevailing tides of non-ethnic hegemony. By subverting the point of view inherent in the construct of the "cultural mosaic," they enable other ways of seeing, a fuller participation in the imaginative life of a diversity of Canadian cultures.

PADMA VISWANATHAN

Padma Viswanathan's Tamil Brahmin family came to Canada from Tamilnadu, south of Madras, India. As she has explained, many of the referents she has used in her play cannot really purport to represent all of India, though they are as Indian as anything else. Each region of India, religious group, linguistic group, is highly distinctive, but they are all equally Indian. Her father studied at a graduate school in North Carolina in the late 1950s, and then moved to Canada. Her mother was active in social justice causes in India, coming of age during the time of early political independence, a time heady with belief in the power of people to effect change peacefully. Padma's political beliefs are close to her mother's, but her reality has been quite different, and that is why *House of Sacred Cows* has an air of forgiveness for "failed activism." She is cynical about the successes of social movements and absolutely unswayed in her belief in their importance. From her mother, Padma also learned the precepts of Hinduism, but not to accept them without question. She returned to India to work with a Ghandian land reform organization at the age of twenty. She has a degree in sociology from the University of Alberta, and as a visiting student at Harvard for a year, she studied "women and the law." At the University of Alberta, she became involved in social-action theatre, and joined The Woman's Circle, a collective led by Jan Selman, creating scripts about women's issues. Believing that she could make more contact with people through theatre than through an academic career, she committed herself to acting and writing. One of her collective theatre projects, *Acting Our Colours*, was devised for a high school anti-racial programme. She co-wrote a video on family violence for the Indo-Canadian Women's Association, entitled *Crossing the Line*, and began an association with Catalyst Theatre as "community outreach coordinator." What she liked about Catalyst was its taste for things that were funny, funky and *not* earnest. With the encouragement of DD Kugler, then director of Northern Light Theatre, Padma developed *House of Sacred Cows* from a short scene she had written during her association with Catalyst. Padma now lives in Montreal, where *House of Sacred Cows* was workshopped by the Teesri Duniya Theatre. She is writing a novel, entitled *Thangam* (Tamil for "gold"), a radio play for the CBC, and a stage play for the Groundswell Festival at Nightwood Theatre in Toronto.

MARTY JACK WOON CHAN

There is a strong autobiographical element in *Mom, Dad, I'm Living with a White Girl*. Like many second-generation Canadians, Marty was afraid of telling his parents that his partner was not from their race and culture, and the play shows "all the things that could have gone wrong." In real life, however, the result was marriage rather than breakup. As the playwright cheerfully admits, he is notorious for exposing skeletons in his family's closet. He has made a living at it. For five years he has written a weekly radio commentary based on his family, entitled "Dim Sum Diary." It chronicles his childhood experiences in Morinville as a member of the only Chinese family in a small Alberta town where his father ran the grocery store. He is currently adapting five episodes for television. The pilot, entitled *The Orange Seed Myth and Other Lies Mothers Tell*, features a family with a fiercely protective mother. It aired on CTV and was nominated in 1998 for a Gemini Award for best writing in a children's or youth programme and awarded the Gold Medal for Best TV Pilot. He has also been nominated several times for the AMPIA award for his dramatic writing and productions. Several of Marty's plays have been produced at the Fringe Theatre Festival in Edmonton including *Snakes and Ladders* (1991), *Something Dead and Evil Lurks in the Cemetery and It's My Dad* (1992), *Confessions of a Deli Boy* (1993), and *The Polaroids of Don* (1994) which, like *Mom, Dad, I'm Living with a White Girl* juxtaposes fantasy and reality. His 1998 Fringe show was *Kick up Your Heels, Nina Zapota*. For one season he played the part of Henry Wong in the television series, *Jake and the Kid*, before he convinced the producers that he was a better writer than an actor, and moved behind the scenes. His educational history includes a B.A. in English and Drama from the University of Alberta, a "Dean's Vacation" from the Engineering Faculty, and a Certificate from the Fine Art of Bartending School. (Marty also confesses to being a "Closet Balloon Animal Maker," "Juggler," and "Owner of Three Cats.")

JONATHAN CHRISTENSON

The co-author and director of *Elephant Wake*, Jonathan Christenson, was born in Saskatoon, Saskatchewan, one of four children whose father was a Lutheran minister, and mother a social worker. He has a B.A. and Master of Fine Arts from the University of Alberta. Jonathan is currently—with Joey Tremblay—the co-artistic director of Catalyst Theatre in Edmonton, Alberta, for which he has co-written several plays which further the mandate of Catalyst to create original Canadian work "that explores new possibilities for the theatrical art form and the process through which it is created." *The Abundance Trilogy* (1997) explores the dark side of life in Alberta through the lives of the misfits, grotesques, and marginalized, and invites the audience to participate as voyeurs of the gothic tales which unfold. According to Jonathan, "the prairies are very exotic—big, lots of magic and intrigue." Other collaborations include *My Perfect Heaven*, *Electra*, and *Songs for Sinners*, an "unmusical" musical which re-enacted the theatre of the absurd: repetitive, meaningless actions punctuated by untalented singing. *The House of Pootsie Plunket* sets the story of Electra in a prairie environment to explore family roots in mythological terms, another attempt "to locate things here . . . to crack what it means to be a Western Canadian," to find or determine a local aesthetic. When *Elephant Wake* travelled to the Edinburgh Fringe Festival in 1997, and to the Brighton Festival the following year, it proved that a very "local" play could reach an international audience. It was highly acclaimed by the critics and awarded an Edinburgh Fringe First Award for Outstanding New Work. For its premiere production at the Edmonton Fringe Festival in 1995, the play received a Sterling Award.

JOEY ROBERT TREMBLAY

Joey Tremblay was awarded a Sterling Award for best actor for his role in *Elephant Wake* during its premiere at the Edmonton Fringe, and a *Stage Magazine* nomination for Best Actor of the Edinburgh Fringe. His performance was lauded in the *Edmonton Journal* reviews as combining "raucous, unquenchable humor and a clown's round-eyed innocence." Jean Claude is "transformed by his tale from village idiot to the last surviving sensitive human being on the face of the planet." With Jonathan Christenson, Joey founded the company which first produced *Elephant Wake*—Noises in the Attic. As co-artistic director of Catalyst Theatre, he continues to write and produce new plays, including *The Abundance Trilogy*, *Songs for Sinners*, and *The House of Pootsie Plunket*. He was born in Birtle, Manitoba, in 1964, and grew up in a very small hamlet called Ste. Marthe in Southeast Saskatchewan, living in the rectory of the church, since the priest and parish had moved to Rocanville. His father was a potash miner, two generations removed from the prairie pioneers who first battled the elements, and whose struggles provide the matrix of his plays. Joey Tremblay received a B.F.A. in Drama from the University of Regina, and a Diploma from the Vancouver Playhouse Acting School.

Anne Nothof
Athabasca University
January 1999

HOUSE OF SACRED COWS

BY PADMA VISWANATHAN

ACKNOWLEDGEMENTS

Though no piece of theatre exists in a vacuum, *House of Sacred Cows* has been particularly and extensively touched by the hands of many professionals. It started in Edmonton, as a twenty minute scene in Catalyst Theatre's playwright's unit, which was headed by Ruth Smillie and Marina Endicott. From there, Northern Light Theatre's DD Kugler commissioned it and became the dramaturg, my indispensable, infuriating, and unmatched companion in the process.

It was workshopped by Toronto's Nightwood Theatre with the generous and gentle advice of Alisa Palmer, Soraya Peerbaye, and Deena Aziz; by the Banff Playwrights Colony, where Marina Endicott put in another appearance, along with Kim McCaw; and, in Ottawa, at the National Arts Centre English Theatre's "On the Verge," for which Lise Ann Johnson did artistic co-ordination. Vanessa Porteous and Lynda Adams were invaluable other eyes in development work and production at Northern Light.

Eight months after the production, Teesri Duniya Theatre of Montreal, to whom the script had been recommended by Sally Han, presented it as a staged reading. The joint efforts of Rahul Varma, Shelley Tepperman, and Svetlana Zylin helped me to process the lessons I learned in production.

The development of this play was funded by the Alberta Foundation for the Arts and Northern Light Theatre.

For the work he does each day, bringing new plays and new writers to the stage, sometimes fighting himself and others to do it, this is for Kugler. For all else, it's dedicated to Ian, Uma, Mom and Dad.

FIRST PERFORMANCE

House of Sacred Cows had its world premiere on 4 December 1997 at the Northern Light Theatre in Edmonton, Alberta.

Amma—Deena Aziz

Guy/Gui—Edward Belanger

Appa—Sama Chakravorty

Anand—Damon D'Oliveira

Orwell—Brian Linds

Leaf—Caroline Livingstone

January—Mieko Ouchi

Junior—Spencer Haynes

Director—DD Kugler

Assistant Director—Vanessa Porteous

Artistic Associate—Lynda Adams

Set/Lighting Design—Mariko Heidelk

Stage Manager—Susan Haynes

Production Manager—Tamara Stabb

Mieko Ouchi as January, Damon D'Oliveira as Anand.
Northern Light Theatre, Edmonton.

Characters

Anand: a slight man, likely not over 30, from anywhere and every-where in urban India; in his third year of an M.A. Dresses in kurta (tunic-like shirt), jeans, and sandals. More than a look or an accent, the necessary quality is that the actor should have the inflections and flair of one who is conjuring the wisdom of the ages, often to his own surprise. Anand never says "no," so he often agrees simply for the sake of not disagreeing. For example, he assents to everything his mother asks, with no real commitment to do any of it.

January: a young Canadian woman

Amma: the ghost of Anand's mother. She wears a six yard sari, wrapped as a Tamil Brahmin woman would, and a huge red bindi (a dot on the forehead that proves she does not consider herself a widow).

Appa: the ghost of Anand's father. He wears a dhoti (a cotton, sheet-like garment wrapped around the waist) and a polyester shirt.

Amma and Appa's clothes may be burned or singed, since they died in a fire. They are lit for an eerie effect and may be at ceiling level. Their feet should not be visible.

Orwell: long time co-op resident, mid-30s

Leaf: co-op resident, late 20s

Guy: 25–30, twin brother of the father of Leaf's son

Gui: 25–30, the father of Leaf's son, swaggering, unkempt. Guy and Gui are played by the same actor.

Junior: Leaf's son, 4 years old, carries a toy airplane

Courier: doesn't matter if s/he shows or not

Characters in the home movie of the founding of the co-op

Sara: January's mother, played by same actor as January, wears a big Indian cotton print dress

Jorge: Sara's boyfriend, played by same actor as Anand

Freakette: played by same actor as Leaf, wearing a sari

Peace-Freak: hippy looking, played by same actor as Guy/Gui

Freaky: psychedelic, sarcastic looking, played by same actor as Guy/Gui

Neighbour: played by same actor as Orwell

Other co-op residents and friends: played by anyone

PLAYWRIGHT'S NOTES ON SETTING

The play takes place sometime in the early to mid '90s, in a Western Canadian city, in a house whose architecture is pre-'70s, so that the details evoke memory.

By the house is a garden with dead but still standing sunflowers and a neglected potted tomato plant with rotten tomatoes still clinging to its stem.

The furniture in the house is hodgepodge.

The snakes which Leaf creates from fabric and stuffing are lying around the house, various lengths and shapes—long, small, tails sewn into mouths, multiple heads, based on real snakes, or fantastic. They are Leaf's craft and her therapy.

The house has four bedrooms, but Leaf's room needs only a door, which can be slammed, and the other three residents need rooms but not (necessarily) doors.

Leaf's door and the area immediately outside it must be fully visible from the living room. There are a couple of steps up to Leaf's room, one of which is broken, and trips the co-op residents.

Anand's room has a balcony. Amma and Appa appear in his room, not on the balcony. Anand's worldly goods consist of a small suitcase held together with electrician's tape and bound with twine, and a stack of books, bound with twine, so he carries the stack by the bow. Each book is individually covered in brown paper and remains so, even while he uses it. He writes his own words on lovely paper, with a quill.

January watches her home movie in her room. When the script says the film is playing, we see a part of it each time, so that the audience has seen the whole film in sequence by the end. There should be a little overlap each time we see a piece of the film, so that there is a sense that it is not too long, and that January plays it over and over. The love scene in Sara's bedroom is not shown until specifically mentioned in the script. Then it is shown without interruption.

The action takes place over eight "days" and seven "nights," with a period "out of time" preceding and following. The "days" and "nights" do not correspond to our own twenty-four hour cycle, nor is the time elapsed between "days" and "nights" uniform. Looking at the action in terms of day and night, though, will help in understanding the rhythms of the co-op universe. Apart from these, demarcated by ✳✳✳, there are no conventional scene separations as such.

The "blue light" signals a moment of transcendence and is an element to be played with in the design, not to be limited by the suggestions in the text. It could even be signified by a music fragment or chord.

PLAYWRIGHT'S NOTES ON THINGS INDIAN

Although concepts and practices are referred to as "Indian," the point of reference is my own—Tamil, Hindu, and, specifically, Brahmin. Since assertions of what is right or true, "Eastern" or "Western," are called into question within the action of the play, it is assumed that the reader will not think any given term applies for all things Indian.

The *Mahabharata* is an ancient Sanskrit epic poem, a story which contains many stories, several of which I have used to illustrate points narrative and pedagogical in the script. I first became familiar with the characters and philosophy through comic book versions of the heroic and puzzling exploits of the Pandavas; many Westerners are aware that the Bhagavad Gita is one episode in the climactic battle. I would advise anyone wanting a sense of the story's scope to read R. K. Narayan's novelization. In the play, January looks at a photo book describing Peter Brook's adaptation for theatre.

A Ganapathi invocation is a prayer to the elephant-headed god of new undertakings. The first production of this play used the first cut from Vadya Lahari's first album, which is on the Music of the World label.

"Namaskaram" is a formal gesture of respect.

"Carnatic" music is the classical music of South India.

"Anna" is Tamil for older brother and "Bhaia" is Hindi for the same. Young people in traditional families use honorifics instead of or in addition to names when addressing their elders.

The starting point for arranging a Hindu marriage, after caste concerns have been addressed, is often the horoscopes of the parties under consideration.

"Sardarji" is literally a respectful way of referring to a Sikh. Colloquially, it is the term for the person who is the butt of jokes in India, jokes that in Canada would have "Ukrainian" or "Newfie" in the place of "Sardarji." Amma makes a racist comment in reference to Anand's quote from Guru Nanak, who was the founder of Sikhism.

"You-only" and "then-only" are hyphenated to indicate that the "only" refers to the word before, not after.

"Tch" is a click of the tongue against the front of the palate. "Chi" is pronounced "chee."

ACT ONE

As house lights dim, Ganapathi invocation.
Blackout.

* * * OUT OF TIME * * *

Change to Pentangle's "Once I had a Sweetheart" as random wisps of January's home movie play. We cannot see January watching.
Sound of Anand's quill and his voice.
Anand: "House of Sacred Cows."

* * * DAY * * *

Lights up.
During Leaf's phone conversation, January hauls out a number of HUGE bags of garbage or stuff for recycling.

Leaf: No, Father, I cannot move back home! I—*My* pride?! . . . You and everyone else in that backwater hellhole think cutbacks are— Listen—. . . This is not about you!! It's people like me who are going to suffer most, Dad, with reduced health care and child care allowances. At least in the co-op—

Anand rings doorbell. It makes a brief noise, but dies while he is pressing it. He presses it again, and gets only a little dead click.

Leaf: Oh, gotta go. *Junior scrambles to get the door; it is a mission for him.* Okay, yeah, love to Mom. Bye.

Anand knocks loudly, Junior struggles with door, Anand opens it.

Anand: *To Junior.* Hello there.

Leaf: Hi. *Junior clings to Leaf's legs.*

Anand: I am Anand. I have come here for the potluck supper—the mutual evaluation opportunity?

January enters at some point.

Leaf: You're a potential member? Christ. Sorry. Come in. There's a message binder, right by the phone, and no one put down that you were coming. We have systems, but . . . Who took the call?

Anand: I am not quite sure. The assignation was suggested by one Miss January.

January: I'm January. Hi, Anand, welcome.

Leaf: You have read your information sheet?

Anand: Information sheet?

Leaf: With your rights and obligations. It's a policy. Any person thinking of joining receives an information package detailing qualifications, procedures, and the nature of this co-operative housing organization. *To January.* You're usually pretty good about this sort of thing. *Back to Anand.* Some people get them and lose them. Or don't bother reading them. I say, if you're so interested—

January: I'll get him his papers, Leaf. *To Anand.* To be honest, I completely forgot you were coming. You know how it gets! Be right back.

She exits. Orwell enters wearing oven mitts.

Orwell: One more's no problem, there's lots. My usual: Tofu Surprise.

Leaf: *To Anand.* How did you hear about the co-op? I put up posters at the anti-racism coalition office.

January re-enters carrying a stapled package of about twenty pages for Anand. Anand hands Junior a pastry box. The child opens it, loses interest, is gone by mid-meeting.

Anand: For my gracious hosts.

Leaf: That's a point for you.

Anand: Milk sweets.

Leaf: Oh, traditional?

Anand: Possibly. I had them often during the festivals of my child-hood. Here, it was an old man, a venerable old man, who sold them to me in the dingy corner store where—

January: Sorry . . . is this everyone?

Leaf: Without an R.S.V.P. notice it's a little hard to tell.

January: It affects our house the most. The three of us are home.

Leaf: No one's using the sign-in-sign-out board.

January: We'd better get going. Orwell, why don't you give Anand the rundown?

Orwell: This is a co-operative living complex. We have four wings: North Wing, Blue Wing, Great Mother Wing, and Che Wing. Everyone takes an equal share of cooking and cleaning, everyone participates in every decision regarding the house.

Anand: This is certainly a most excellent ideal of democracy.

Orwell: We try. The, you know, best part about living like this?— in a community?—is the opportunity for collective sharing and collective action—

Leaf: Like the extended family situation we've lost in the West—

Orwell: With capitalism and stuff—

Leaf: It's time to reclaim—

Orwell: Communities like ours are the final bulwark against the ever-present threat of exploitation and loneliness—

January: *Gently.* You guys . . . *Indicates pages.* Don't we have to ask some questions?

Leaf: Yeah, can you cook?

Anand: When I came to the West, I had never in my life cooked. Then one evening, I was walking to Mr. Submarine. I am a graduate student. I had in my pocket seven dollars, not a cent more. A man stopped me on the street—a white man, with such very dirty hair and nails. "I need a couple a bucks, man, I need ta eat."

Back home this is a daily occurrence: lepers, small children holding the hands of smaller children . . . Of course, I would feel badly. In my heart. But I am a practical man. I give, but I cannot give to each and every one who asks. This time, this time in the West, I could not refuse. I could not let this man go hungry. So I asked him, "Can I cook for you?" Just like you, he asked, "I don't know, man, can you?" So cheeky, he was.

With my seven dollars, I bought rice, vegetables, Patak's curry paste. I have never eaten such a terrible meal—it was wonderful! I had cooked for my guest! We smoked his two cigarettes and talked and talked. He could have been a great man. So sad. We fell asleep talking. In the morning: gone. Yes, yes, I will cook for you.

All are spellbound.

January: Maybe I'll show Anand the room he'll be in. *January and Anand walk to Anand's room.* The guy who lived in the room before renounced all worldly attachment. *As Anand's foot goes through a stair.* Watch it! I'm so sorry, are you okay?

Anand: No permanent damage, I'm certain.

January: That's a note for the maintenance committee.

Anand: Will this former co-habitant now wander as an ascetic, pursuing enlightenment by his yoga of renunciation?

January: It would be great if he got enlightened. Last time, he mostly got stranded. Shivering and penniless in northern B.C. His ex-wife rescued him.

They step into the room. A scream of pain and frustration is heard from Orwell offstage.

January: Oh God.

Runs off. Anand explores a bit. Tamil film music, Amma and Appa appear. Anand sees them and does namaskaram: bending to touch the region of their feet, then his eyes, and putting his hands together.

Amma: Appa must speak with you.

Anand: Oh, yes.

Amma: *To Appa.* Ask him. Ask him how much longer until he finishes his M.A.

Appa: Humph, harumph.

Amma: You-only must tell him to hurry up and study. How many more responsibilities! Tell him.

Appa: Humph. Responsibilities! No, hah! Young people of today! When I was their age . . . heh, heh . . . Lovely times, what ho! Rowing matches, high tea, high jinks, ahhh . . . English bastards.

January knocks and enters. She sees Amma and Appa. Amma sees her.

Amma: Anand, my only son. Why are you shifting to this place? You will be living in one house with all sorts of females and whatnot.

Anand: No, Amma, no whatnot, whatsoever. Amma, I must move. The university would grant me residence for two years only.

Amma: Two year course, is it not? Two years finished—and now shifting! Why? Why you are not coming home, Anand, as you promised?

Anand: Amma, I still have writing to do, Amma. My thesis.

Amma: Thes-is! That-is! Thes-is, that-is . . . Everything only taking more time. Appa and I are waiting so long. You must complete your studies. You must find husbands for your sisters, you must then marry.

Anand: Yes, Amma, I must—

Amma: Then-only we can go to the next life.

Anand: I must relieve you of the weight of these responsibilities.

Appa: Ooohh, the weight of history, sticking feet to the ground, keeping us standing, up.

Amma: Okay, okay, see this place. We will be still waiting. Waiting.

Anand: Yes, Amma, you are very patient.

Appa: Harumph. We . . . are famous for incomparable patience . . . No other age or civilization . . . tops us.

They disappear.

January: Did you . . . invoke them?

Anand: They came, simply. To advise me.

January: You needed advice?

Anand: Apparently I did.

January: Would it be rude to . . . ask how they died?

Anand: Riots.

January: Oh, I'm sorry.

Anand: Just before my scheduled departure from India, Mahapsara, the Chief Minister of our home state, died. Tragic, I tell you. From screen goddess, she had become state goddess. Above all that is sacred in India are cows and movie stars. And when movie stars become politicians . . . Mahapsara had installed her own fourteen foot likeness at every roadway and state gathering. Her MPs would prostrate before her, her pudgy features conferred blessings on all.

On this ill-starred day, Mahapsara and her entourage were en route to one function. Delays had been caused by a herd of cattle taking a snack between the ties of the commuter train line. Train was stopped, engineer was beating and screaming at the cows with utmost respect. But Mahapsara's car would stop for no one and nothing. So-so suddenly, her car crashed . . . into the unmoving train.

Tragedy! An idol lost! Madras went mad, I tell you! People jump-ing off rooftops, overturning taxis. Setting fire to my parents' building.

January: I'm so sorry.

Anand: What is to be, will be, and to be destroyed, will be destroyed. There is nothing to be done.

January: I wish I could believe that.

Anand: Do your own good parents come to visit you here?

January: No. *Steps out onto the balcony; sun is setting.* There's a won-derful feeling of solitude out here, isn't there?

Anand: It is solitude you desire?

January: No. I've spent plenty of time alone. I don't mind living with other people.

Anand: Not once in my life have I been left alone. My family and friends are so attached to me. In India, nobody lives alone, nobody goes to places alone, nobody eats alone.

January: Crowded country.

Anand: Very true, very true. And from constant crowding, the exaltation of constant companionship. Back home, it is so common to criticize Western families as far too independent and individualistic. As you see, my dear parents assured by their death that I would never be alone, even in this Western waste land. Not a chance of solitude in an Indian family. Not a chance.

January: Not everyone in the West is individualistic. People in the co-op think there is something to be achieved by living communally.

Anand: Oh, yes. Very good. What is it you are wanting to achieve?

January: I don't know . . . a utopian society? Where everyone participates and is heard.

Leaf shoves her position paper, about ten pages, stapled, under each bedroom door and leaves a stack by the phone for the duration of the play.

Anand: The real democracy.

January: Utopian, right? . . . and sado-masochistic. We vote on everything.

Anand: But you would not live here if you did not have a vote.

January: Sure we would, it's cheap . . . Okay, oppression by democracy has got to be better than bald tyranny.

Anand: Oh, yes, how well I know it. Truly, January, whether you hold your nose like this or reach all the way around your head like so, it's all the same. You're still holding your nose!

January: Exactly. *Gazing off balcony.* The co-op was started twenty-five years ago. It must have meant a lot to those people, then. I want to get it back on track, back to what they intended. *Off: dinner bell rings.* Look. So peaceful.

Orwell: *From way offstage.* Tofu Surprise!

Anand: *Indicating the scene off the balcony.* The city is cloaked in twilight. All our earthly weights will soon be dreams. *Holding out his* *hand to January, who takes it.* Let us join with the formless, the timeless. In this moment, we need not have any answers.

They make as if to step off the balcony, lights fade on them, and a beating of wings is heard, and song fragment or chord.

NIGHT

Orwell plays a computer game alone in his room. Something goes wrong with it, he pulls out a screwdriver and fixes it—very quickly—then goes on playing.

January watches the film to Pentangle's "Once I had a Sweetheart."

The film shows:

—some rapid cuts, while someone swings the camera around, trying to figure it out.

—in front yard, Sara presenting the new house with a grand gesture; camera takes in the house with a couple of wide sweeps, then focuses on a sunflower and a thriving tomato plant.

—walk through the house to the back yard.

—inside and out, many people running and dancing, could be people playing music, could be guitars, harps, tablas, sitar, African drums, others blowing bubbles, doing palm reading, building houses of tarot cards, raggedy looking kids, etc.

DAY

Leaf bustles around getting tea set up for about fifteen people. January enters. Each has a copy of Leaf's position paper. They sit in the living room.

Leaf: What time is it?

Doorbell rings and dies mid-buzz.

January: Ten to. *Answers door.* Hi, Anand. Got your stuff? *Anand has his suitcase and books.* Great. I haven't had a chance to clean the room too well yet . . .

Anand: No, no, no, certainly, no inconvenience.

January: We're having an *ad hoc* committee meeting this morning to discuss a new, or, actually, a revival of one of the founding policies that was never implemented.

Orwell enters living room, also carrying Leaf's memo, sits.

Orwell: Oh, well, guess I didn't need to hurry. What time is it?

January: Twenty minutes late. Anyone do a phone around last night? Who was planning to come? *All look at each other blankly.* I'll go make some calls.

January goes to phone.

Leaf: I heard Che Wing wanted to come, but the march against, or is it for, no it must be against the U.S. assistance in, or, invasion of, Nigeria is on today. I think most of them felt that was a higher priority. My son, he's four, he's still sleeping, but he's been going to rallies since he was born. Living in the co-op has been so good for him. He's exposed to different—

Orwell: I totally agree, non-formal education is so important, not the educational institutions, they're bad, but popular education—

January returns.

January: No one's picking up the phone in North Wing or Che Wing, and all the Blue Wing members are apparently home but vomiting uncontrollably.

The doorbell rings and loud knocking follows. January gets it.

Guy: Hi.

Leaf stares in shock.

Orwell: Hi.

Leaf: Guy . . .

Guy: I'm living in the co-op. Just like you and Junior.

January: Great. Glad you could make it. Let's start.

Leaf picks up an apparently finished snake, wraps a new cloth around it—a new "skin" and starts sewing. January hands out agendas.

January: I know it's not quorum, but we can still have the discussion and just say that the decisions are non-binding. Since the secretary is coping with botulism at Blue Wing, could someone here take minutes? Orwell?

Orwell: Uhh, no. I want to, but, just, I've done it before and I can never read my writing . . .

January: Oh, come on, I'll help you type them up later.

Orwell: . . . all right.

January: Ho-kay, first item on the agenda. Acceptance of the agenda. Have I got someone to make the motion? *Orwell raises his hand.* A seconder? *Leaf looks around, raises her hand.* Comments?

Guy: This was printed on a really crappy printer.

Orwell: It's no luxury model but it gets the job done.

Guy: You can barely read it.

Orwell: Look, I built that printer, okay? *Quiet.* And the computer and the modem. Out of reclaimed parts from dumpsters—you wouldn't believe what people throw away.

Guy: Like crappy printers?

January: Uh—what is the feeling of the group on this agenda right now? Is it good enough that we can get on with the meeting?

Everyone looks at Guy.

Guy: Yeah, I guess.

January: Great! As you can see, there's actually only one other item on the agenda, that's the policy proposal I suggested at the AGM, *Leaf ready to jump in,* but first, we have some new faces, so maybe we could do brief introductions. *Nods at Anand to start.*

Anand: My name is Anand. I am filled with joy at the prospect of taking part in this great social experiment. I come from India, where democracy is still fresh. We never take for granted the opportunity to participate in the running of our states. It seems every parent wants the child to join government service. The bureaucracy is thoroughly corrupt, but, like an old hornet's nest— indestructible. Still, we believe in democracy and, *Catching January's eye* . . . I am very happy to be here.

January: Thanks, Anand. *Looks at Orwell, who says nothing.* Orwell?

Orwell: *Still a bit hurt.* Well, um, I'm Orwell.

January: And you live in . . .

Orwell: Here. Great Mother Wing.

January: Thanks. Go ahead.

Guy: I'm Guy Champlaine. I just moved into Che Wing.

January: Thanks. So . . . I'm January, and I chair the board, which means I'm a member of the finance committee. I also co-ordinate the maintenance committee and membership committee, I co-co-ordinate the policy committee with the co-op secretary, I'm starting an education-slash-advocacy committee, um, did I forget anything?

Orwell: Social committee.

January: And social committee. So come to me with needs in any of those areas. New members should find a committee to join. *To Orwell.* Actually, could I have a special reminder in the minutes about committee time? *To Guy and Anand.* It's an aspect of the commitment that's so often forgotten, even by longtime members. *Orwell, guilty, returns to scribbling. January looks to Leaf.*

Leaf: I'm Leaf, as you all know, and a mum, as you know—

January: Good. Thanks everyone. So—

Guy: Leaf, I need you.

Leaf: You're crazy.

Guy: I need you.

Leaf: You're confused.

Guy: I would make a good father to your child.

Leaf: My child has a father.

January: Do you two need some privacy?

Leaf: No. This is settled. Guy just wants to be with me because he has unresolved feelings about his brother.

Guy: That's got nothing to do with it. I love you!

Leaf: You can't love me! You're genetically incapable! You want to possess me.

Guy: And I know you love me.

January: Hey. If she says she doesn't love you—

Leaf: Maybe I do love you. I was confused, too, I still am. It won't work. Your twin brother is the father of my child!

January: Oh. Are you sure you don't want to go somewhere on your own, and talk this through?

Leaf: There's nothing to talk about.

January: Let's get on with it, then. This is the proposal. It's not a motion, I withdrew it as a motion, but this is the idea: Moved that . . . Sorry. Proposed that monthly housing charges, in landlord parlance, rents, should be twenty-five percent of the monthly income of any given co-op member, with an adjustment for size of room occupied.

Anand: I have long felt sympathy for this stirring maxim: to each according to his needs, from each according to his abilities.

January: I think a lot of people feel that way, even if their faith has been a little shaken by communist fallout.

Leaf: All of my comments are there, in the memo I handed round to everyone yesterday. I took copies to the other wings as well.

January: Mm-hm. Any responses?

Orwell: I, uh, I think this issue is really, it's really worth discussing.

January: Any particular point you want to raise?

Orwell: Well, I think you sort of said it too, January, the other night, that we don't want to, like, penalize people or anything, you know, who happen to be earning a decent wage—

Leaf: Excuse me, January, but I do have a response to that in my memo.

January: Which was . . . ?

Leaf: *Sometime during this speech, the sleepy child comes down from Leaf's room and climbs into her lap.* Right here on page four: "At present, it's the poor and others who are systemically excluded from employment and sources of wealth who are being penalized in the housing market. Single mothers, like myself, who can claim nothing from their children's fathers, maybe because these men are untraceable, those single mothers, like me, have to struggle on a daily basis to make ends meet. The government is cutting off child support, and free and accessible health care, but the co-op is supposed to be a place where these problems are acknowledged, where some solutions can be found. The proportional rent policy was one of the co-op's founding policies. It doesn't punish the rich, it acknowledges that some of us have it harder. . . . " It's all here, in black and white, I don't have to read it all over again.

January: Those are very powerful, very eloquent statements, Leaf. Does anyone have any argument?

Orwell: Those are really good points, but, um, it still doesn't seem like quite a great idea, to hang rent on income. *To January.* Didn't you, or someone, might have said, that, like, you don't want this to turn into a place where more stable people won't live. There's got to—

Leaf: More stable people?

Orwell: Just people with more stable incomes, I mean. You don't want a ghetto of—

Leaf: A ghetto. It's not bad enough there are no jobs, I'm raising . . . Did you even read my memo before coming here? *Silence.* Did you?

Orwell: Yeah! Well, parts, and . . .

Leaf: *Gasping in disbelief.*

January: It's really long, Leaf.

Leaf: I don't have time for this. I clearly state my opinion and no one's interested.

January: We're having the meeting, Leaf, I—

Leaf: A meeting? When I bring my contribution to the table and nobody even reads it? Call me when I'm not the only one participating in this so-called democracy.

Leaf storms out to her room, carrying her child; Guy charges after her, gets slammed out of her bedroom, leaves.

January: *To herself.* True, we don't have quorum . . . but we could start building consensus. That way as more join the group, their opinions could be incorporated into the emerging group decision.

Sure, January, but in order to build consensus, all parties must have an equal commitment to working through conflict. Good point. Do we have that commitment? We're committed to living co-operatively, and communal living naturally engenders difference, ergo we must all be committed to working through issues as they arise.

Glad to hear that, because I have found the process of finding consensus can be a really bonding experience. *Anand clears tea tray to kitchen.* That would be ideal, but there is a danger of alienating the few whose opinions may be far from the emerging consensus. But, we are mature adults and ultimately trying to achieve the same thing. And with skilled facilitation, no result is impossible.

To Orwell. I'd say this meeting is over. For today. Thanks for coming. I'd appreciate it if you could type up the minutes, such as they are, and make sure each wing gets a copy. I'm going for a walk.

She leaves. Anand walks through with sandwich.

Orwell: *Scrutinizing his notes.* I didn't get any of that.

Anand continues up to his room with luggage and sandwich. Puts away things, takes out magazine or newspaper, and eats while reading. After he has enjoyed this for a minute or so, Amma and Appa appear to some austere Carnatic music.

Amma: O, Anand, what are you eating?

Anand: A sandwich, Amma.

Amma: Remember what I said would happen if you eat meat.

Anand: O, I remember, Amma.

Amma: My only son must not reincarnate as a pig.

Anand: Even Vishnu had one avatar as wild boar, Amma.

Appa: A bore! But we tolerated. Such a perennial bore.

Anand: Perennial, yes—what of vegetables? Eating vegetable life must equally be an act of evil.

Amma: No, no, no. Plants are there for eating only.

Anand: What if I came back as a squash or a pea plant, Amma?

Amma: Doesn't happen.

Anand: Then, animals. Other castes eat animals, animals eat other animals—

Amma: Are you a child to ask such questions, Anand?

Anand: Even great Guru Nanak says, "We are born from flesh, we suckle at flesh, and as flesh we die and decay. . . . Why shun the flesh?"

Amma: You can quote Sardarji to me!? You are converting to be a Sikh?

Anand: No Amma, no, no, no . . . *Looking longingly at sandwich and reading stuff.*

Amma: I-only fed you, I-only nursed you when you were a this big baby. Let them go and do all every filthy-filthy thing. I am telling you—

Anand: We must consume life to live. This results in accumulation of karma, but it is a necessary evil—

Appa: The necessary evil. But they employed us and gave us pants to wear.

Amma: Show me the sandwich, Anand.

Anand: Amma!!

Amma: Show it. *Anand obeys.* Meat!! Meat!!

Appa: "The poor benighted Hindoo / He does the best he kin do / Sticks to his caste / From first to last / And for trousers just lets his skin do." Kipling couldn't have said it better.

Anand: Amma, no, Amma, this is some . . . imitation, made from soybeans and colourings, to look and taste like meat.

Amma: Why?

Anand: I don't know. *Looks at sandwich, offers it.* Bite?

Amma: Chi! *Sniffingly rejects his offer.*

Amma and Appa vanish. Anand sighs, goes to his desk, dips quill, begins writing.

Anand: The funeral pyre does not address the body. It is a vehicle for transport of the soul. The body is symbolic, a burnt offering. Then again, fire, by following its nature, devours the sticks of wood that gave it life. *Pauses in writing.* So, Agni, god of fire and devoted son, is said to have eaten his parents.

Flare of blue light as Anand resumes writing.

Leaf chasing her child toward her room.

Leaf: That is not a gun! How many times have I told you that guns are a symbol of violence and this is a zero-tolerance zone? It's a plane! *He reaches room first, slams door, locks it.* Oh, fuck. Open that door! *No answer.* Well, you're in there until you stop that, understand? *January enters.* Am I a bad mother?

January: Of course not.

Leaf: I didn't think so.

Gun noises. Junior exits room, runs from one end of the house to the other. He zooms past Leaf and January, shooting at them. Leaf just looks at him in resignation, then picks up a snake and starts working on it.

Leaf: I thought the co-op would be more supportive . . .

January: Leaf, come on. The co-op wants to support you—

Leaf: I need help now! . . . My father, he wants me to come and live with him, in that miserable little town. I can't go and live there, everyone votes wrong. But I'm so broke.

January: Did anything come of the harassment complaint?

Leaf: No, Brad's got a scared new waitress every week. No one else will speak up. They're all scared of getting stuck with no job and no references. Like me!

Junior has heard his mom being upset. Flies his plane in—as a plane— and hugs her.

January: Let's work on your resumé together, tonight, on Orwell's computer. I'll baby-sit tomorrow while you take it around. You can use me as a reference. And I've been thinking, you could also look into selling your snakes somewhere.

Leaf: I should, yeah. Thanks. Really. *Anand enters.* You realize, Anand, the proportional rent policy could go a long way toward attracting visible minorities. The co-op's already so white, and obviously a lot of people here want it middle class . . . Omigod, my Goddess workshop! Can you still look after—

January: Sure, leave him to me.

Leaf: His Aladdin tape's in the VCR. *To Anand.* Racist, sexist, I know, it was a gift. And we talked about it. Bye, sweetie, January's looking after you 'til I get back.

Junior: When are you coming home?

Leaf: Around five.

Junior: *To January.* Are we flying?

January: Are you airworthy?

Leaf slips out.

Junior: No, I'm Noseworthy.

They both find this very funny, no one else must.

January: Pleased to meet you, I'm Brainworthy.

Junior: Pleased to meet you, I'm . . . did Mommy go already?

January: She'll be back really soon. Why don't you fuel up and I'll meet you on the backyard runway in a few minutes.

Junior takes off.

Anand: His father is . . . ?

January: Long gone.

Anand: And here in this community you all take a part in bringing up this fatherless child.

January: Whoa . . . he's still her kid. I call him the Leaflet. And he is a great little guy, considering.

Anand: And your own good mother? She is nearby to take care of you?

January: *A cloud passes over her face.* No, she's out east. She was one of the founders. Of this great co-operative institution.

Anand: That is most certainly one outstanding achievement! She will be twice immortalized—by her beautiful daughter and this great contribution to social welfare and well being. *January runs to the door.* She must be very proud that you are now treading the path she cleared.

January: *At door.* Hm, got to get to that weatherproofing soon. *Returns with the mail, holds out an Indian aerogram.* Letter for you.

Anand takes the letter, looks at the return address.

Anand: *To January.* Would you read it to me, please?

January: Me? If you're sure it's not private.

Anand: Tch. Privacy is a falsehood. Do we not share the same joys and troubles? The letter is from my sister. It would be a great pleasure for me to hear her words spoken by your melodious voice.

January opens the letter.

January: "My dear Anand bhaia: I guess you are now in your new digs? How exciting for you. Hope we will soon see photos of the accommodations and your friends or roommates."

Paragraph. "Okay, no more beatings about the bushes. Rajan Uncle has given me an ultimatum. Of course, he sees it as a favour. Uncle says if you do not write and say you have found a husband for me in Canada or come back soon and secure someone for me here, he himself will initiate the proceedings. He has a copy of my horoscope, and several good prospects. Anna, what can I do? I can't tell him to stop. You know my feelings for Ravi. He and I can only marry with your support. Please, please call me as soon as you can and advise me. I am counting on you."

New paragraph. "I am sure Uma would send her love and respects. At the moment, she is at a disco club, as every night. She is still securing top marks. Vidya Aunty is well. I'm sure she would send her love and kisses if she were awake. She is still the sweetest old soul. In any case, I am *eagerly anticipating your phone call.*"

That's underlined three times and is in a bubble like in a comic strip and it's coming out of the head of, oh, I guess it's supposed to be her self portrait, and . . . she's got a noose around her neck! Anand, what . . . is this pretty serious?

Anand: *Unhappily.* Marriage is ever a life and death situation.

January: "Yours aff'ly, Lakshmi." Your younger sister?

Anand: Mm. We could be separated by a much larger earth than this, still I am the only one she comes to. Now we are apart. Who will protect her?

January: Sounds like the rest of the family wants to protect her.

Anand: Who will protect her from the rest of the family?

January: You're not helpless. The phone's right there.

Anand: How can I advise her? I am not an elder person. There is a saying in Hindi, "A child must be led by the thumbs until she has the experience to lead herself." *January gasps.* Hindi is not my mother tongue.

January: "Paint as you like and die happy." Henry Miller said that.

Anand: Tagore! "Come and take your seat in the bosom of the limitless, my child. At sunrise open and raise your heart like a blossoming flower and at sunset bend your head and in silence complete the worship of the day."

January: Stop deflecting! Your little sister needs your help. Urgently. Am I right?

Anand: Quite right. My parents are also stuck and needing my help to ensure the welfare and well-being of their children: give them education and spouses, make good decisions on their behalf—

January: A grown woman can make decisions for herself.

Anand: Of course she can. And in so doing, deny her parents their divinely granted privilege and duty.

January: And now you have to do their duty for them?

Anand: Precisely.

January: What about your sister's happiness?

Anand: What is happiness?

January: Different things for different people.

Anand: Very true, excellent. And for you right now, January, what is happiness?

January: Lots of things. I'm discovering.

Anand: *Paraphrasing her to suit his argument.* You do not yet know what will bring you happiness. The parent will make the best choice. Is this commune not your mother's gift to you? *January shrugs.* She had a vision for your future.

January: She couldn't have known what my needs would be. The world's more complicated . . . Nice job—changing the subject. *Orwell enters, coming home from the office.* I know an Indian woman who consented to an arranged marriage and she's quite happy. She says probably half of arranged marriages work out, same as Western marriages. Fine. But your sister's not happy with the arrangements being made for her. *Indicates letter.* Horoscopes?

Anand: I am not yet one with the immutable. How can I judge the methods and traditions of thousands of years? Our Indian mind should turn now to the folly of freedom?

Orwell: Wow.

January: What "folly"? What about India's whole freedom struggle? Independence, Gandhi, and all that. It's so inspiring.

Anand: Oh-ho, India gained democracy, not freedom. From your experience here in this great democratic experiment, you yourself have told me, that these two are not the same.

January: *Your* sister is asking *you* to stand up for her, and you're not planning to. This isn't the last you'll hear from me on this topic. *Exits.*

Anand: *To Orwell.* January is so very much like my own dear, delightful sisters. Tell me, you handsome fellow, are you still without a tender helpmeet to share all of your days and nights and to dream with you?

Orwell: Is this a proposal?

NIGHT

January alone in her room, with the hiccups, trying unsuccessfully to control them.

Anand and Orwell walk in otherwordly pools of light as from street lamps. They look totally alone together.

Anand: What are you looking for in this great co-operative enterprise?

Orwell: I think, it's nice to live together with other people. When you live alone you can get too set in your ways, narrow-minded, and stuff.

Anand: So true. In India, we never have the chance to live alone and fall into these sorts of unrecommendable habits.

Orwell: I know it sounds funny, but if I had the chance for an arranged marriage, I would almost take it.

Anand: You would prefer a marriage arranged by your family?

Orwell: Not exactly, but, sort of, yeah . . . lots of people in the West just never have to get to know someone that well.

Anand: Oh, so? Even in this communal ideal, this extended family set-up?

Orwell: Even here. You can still be really alone.

Anand: But you are free to come and go, no responsibilities . . .

Orwell: Oh, I believe in freedom, and choice, and . . . except sometimes, I sort of, catch myself wondering if freedom is overrated. If you have to give up your freedom to have someone special, someone nice to share your life, maybe you would choose to do that, if you had the choice.

Anand: You are not the freedom fighter, my friend. You are the lost romantic.

Orwell: Am I lost?

Anand: *Touching his face affectionately.* Hopelessly.

Blue light. Orwell might just groan slightly.

* * * DAY * * *

Junior runs around the house, flying his airplane

Junior: January January January January January!

He bursts into Anand's room. Appa is enjoying some solitude.

Appa: Oh-ho, chhota sahib!

Junior: Hi.

Appa looks at him, directly.

Anand and Orwell play chess in living room, very absorbed. Leaf enters, carrying a bag of resumés, and slumps into a living-room chair.

Orwell: Hi, how're you doing.

Leaf gives him a very dirty look, then ignores him.

Junior: D'you know how to fly?

Appa: I have never been in an aeroplane.

Junior: Anand came in an airplane. Are you Anand's dad? My dad flies.

Appa: Once, I too could fly, but then I realized it was just a dream, illusion, and I fell from the sky, heavy with enlightenment.

Junior: My dad flew too high and far away and got lost. But I'm going to find him, pretty soon.

Appa: My son was once suspected of flying. I must remember to ask him sometime. I must ask my son if he flies.

Junior: I saw a story about a boy who could fly, but my mother told me not to try it.

Appa: Ah, what son would tell his father, "Father, I do fly"? But— little man—maybe you can help me remember how.

Blue light.

January enters living room with a big blue bowl of hot water and bottle of Compound W.

January: From now on, we disinfect that bathtub. With something toxic. This is the third wart I've addressed this month. Someone in this house is a carrier. *Soaks foot.*

Leaf: I am so depressed.

January: Any luck?

Leaf: Nope.

January: . . . little one's napping.

Silence as everyone does their thing.

Orwell: *To January.* What are you doing?

Anand moves a chess piece.

January: Treating warts.

Orwell moves chess piece in response to Anand's move.

Anand: O-ho, my clever friend!! I am Arjuna's young son in the Mahabharata, who knows only how to infiltrate the enemy's formation, but not how to escape it. Like Arjuna's dastardly cousins, you have trapped me!!

Orwell: *To January.* Can I see? *She shows him.* They hurt?

January: Yeah.

Orwell: When you step on them, or all the time?

January: Mostly . . . *A moment of realization.* Why?

Orwell: I think I'm sure mine aren't contagious any more.

January: How long . . . I can't believe you didn't warn us.

Orwell: I guess, I sort of got used to them.

January: Have you got lots?

Orwell: I . . . can't really tell. It's pretty acrobatic, you know, holding your foot to see, and count, and everything.

January: *Imitation Indian accent.* Whether you hold your foot like this, or reach all the way around and grab it like this, it's all the same . . . get rid of them.

Orwell: How?

January: Burn them off.

Orwell: Burn . . . ?

January: *Applies stuff while singing.* Burn, baby, burn, Disco Inferno . . .

Leaf: *Sighs, gets up.* God, it would be nice to hear something meaningful discussed for a change. *Goes to her room.*

January: . . . sorry. Obviously you're not as susceptible to warts as the rest of us.

Leaf closes her door.

Orwell: I can't say a thing *to* her, *around* her . . . We've got to do something.

January: "We"? *To Anand.* What do you post-colonial types have to say about fighting other people's wars?

Orwell: I have to deal with her all by myself?

January: No, I meant, we can't fix what's wrong with her life.

Anand: It is a great conflict. My own dear Aunty Vidya . . . she used to sweep the cupboard and find big red ants carrying off the sugar. She killed them, but each time she hit one with the broom she would say the name of God, "Ram-Ram," so the insect would be blessed and reborn into a better life. My mother would get furious: "You can kill this bug or you can bless it! You are not God who can do both!"

Ah—but every morning, Aunty would sweep the courtyard and draw a huge, symmetrical design to honour the household goddess. Always in rice flour, never in synthetic powders or chalk. Vidya Aunty would ask me, "Do you know why you must always make kolam in rice flour?" Do you? *They don't.* "To feed the ants. They are our guests, they must not leave hungry."

Leaf goes to the basement without a word .

January: *Clarifying.* So, it's good to invite guests and feed them. But thieves should die. But be reborn into a better life.

Anand: My Vidya Aunty has a very complex mind.

January: No doubt.

Anand: Even though she left school to marry at the age of eight years.

January: Eight?

Anand: She married my father's eldest brother and was widowed by the age of ten. She had never lived with her husband, but when she came of age, she left her own family and came to stay with us. Such was a woman's lot at that time.

January: Thank God times have changed.

Anand: Indeed. Thank God.

January: Thank God times have changed and maybe your sister can have the choice your aunt never had.

Anand: My sister has finished her college education and has already had many more opportunities than the ladies of the previous generation.

January: You chose. Even though your parents died, you did what you wanted. You came to Canada, instead of staying in India to look after the family affairs.

Anand: I followed the advices of family elders—that I could make better opportunities for myself abroad.

January: You know that's what you really wanted to do.

Leaf returns from basement with small overnight bag.

Leaf: Look. *Orwell takes bowl out to kitchen.* I left a note in the message binder two days ago: that whoever's stuff was in front of my luggage downstairs, it had to be moved.

January: *Rising.* I think that's mine.

Anand seizes the opportunity and leaves.

Leaf: I've done it already.

January: *Sitting again.* Are you going somewhere?

Leaf: My dad's taking Junior down for a visit.

January: Great. You can use some time for yourself. And you're okay with that, with Junior under his influence?

Leaf: Yes and no. I feel like . . .

Guy reappears.

Guy: Leaf! Leaf, it's me, Gui, the father of your child!!

Leaf: Come off it, Guy, I can tell you two apart.

Guy: But genetically, I could be the father of your child. He's our immaculate conception. You are my Madonna.

Leaf: Go home.

Goes to her room, shuts door, Guy leaves.

Anand in his room pacing and writing.

Anand: Yet the roles of fathers are never clear. Great Vyasa unofficially fathered his brother's sons, Pandu and Dhritharashtra. Pandu's sons, the Pandavas, were sired by gods. And while Dhritharashtra begat his own hundred offspring, he offered them none of a father's moral authority. When Vyasa narrated the great story of Pandu's sons, and their battles with their hundred evil cousins, his scribe was Ganesha, whose mother created him from mud while her husband was away. When a father can be so much and so little, how much more or less a son?

January picks up a book (The Making of Peter Brook's Mahabharata, *say). She turns on the stereo, something lively (suggested: Prince Nico Mbarga, "Sweet Mother") and reclines on the couch. Orwell returns with big, blue bowl of hot water. He sits, soaks his foot, starts humming along, not really in tune, not very loud, not even continuously, just sort of humming. It's almost like a mannerism. After a minute or two, January looks at him. He points to the bottle of Compound W as if to ask, can I use that? She indicates, go right ahead. He picks it up and keeps humming. She sighs and keeps reading. She gets up and goes. He smiles at her as she leaves. He is nodding and enjoying the music, his foot in the bowl.*

Leaf walks Junior to the door.

Leaf: No, somehow I don't think it's too likely grandpa can fly.

Junior: Maybe I can help him, like I helped Anand's dad.

Leaf: Maybe.

Junior: At first, he was a little scared, but then he remembered how. He's pretty good, just needs practice.

Leaf: Oh.

Junior: He said I should keep on doing it, so I don't forget how. I could teach you sometime, Mommy.

Leaf: That would be wonderful, honey. Grandpa's waiting in the car. So, be good, don't give Grandma any trouble, and if Grandpa starts putting poor people down . . .

Junior: Ignore him.

Leaf: That's my guy. Kiss Mommy. Love you. See you in a few days.

Junior leaves, Leaf heads for her room, sees Orwell, speeds up, shuts herself in. The door opens just wide enough for her arm to hang a DO NOT DISTURB *sign on the knob. She slams the door shut again.*

NIGHT

Appa practices flying.

January watches film to Pentangle's "Once I had a Sweetheart."

The film shows:

—inside and out, many people running and dancing, could be people playing music, could be guitars, harps, tablas, sitar, African drums, others blowing bubbles, doing palm reading, building houses of tarot cards, raggedy looking kids, etc.

—inside: Freakette, kissing Peace-Freak on one side and someone else on the other side of her.

—in backyard, someone brings out bottles of beer, indicates s/he brewed it at home, maybe there are big handwritten labels on the bottles.

—Sara gestures the camera over, she has the documents, the certificate of incorporation which she displays proudly to the camera, then starts to put in a frame.

DAY

Sunrise: Anand and Orwell performing Sun salutation. They look as though they are beneath a tree or in a grove. They perform it one full round in silence. They are both a bit sleepy and trying not to show it. Orwell may be trying to dress a little like Anand or otherwise look like him.

Orwell: I guess it's pretty early for this. Not that . . . I mean, I do it all the time, but what with . . . daylight savings and everything . . .

They assume Lotus pose and do breathing exercises like Anuloma Viloma, Brahmari, Sitkari, Sithali.

Orwell: What is yoga?

Anand: Yoga is of threefold types—action, knowledge, and devotion. Each is equally a path to the One, but for each of us, one path is more equal than the others.

Orwell: I should, I'd like to do it every day. You do, right?

Anand: When I fall asleep at night, I try to reassure my limbs they will be useful in the morning.

They stay in Lotus pose, doing breathing exercises, a few moments more, break at the same time, giddy from the extra oxygen, and try to assume the Bridge pose. Neither is all that good at it. They hold it for some time, then lie in Corpse pose to rest.

Orwell: Anand? Are you staying? That is, are you going to stay?

Anand: Each of us dwells simply in the city of nine gates.

Orwell: Where?

Anand: This mortal body. Nine entrances and exits. Traffic in and out, breath in and out, sound, taste, sensation . . .

They take Cobra pose. Blue light glows more strongly.

Orwell: Cobra pose.

Anand: Yes. The serpent is Shakti, power, coiled at the base of the spine.

Orwell: Coiled.

Anand: Dormant.

Orwell: Dormant.

Anand: You can awaken it, Orwell.

Orwell: Shakti power?

Anand: Energy, of the first type.

Orwell: Meaning?

Anand: Many things. Bliss. Liberation. Sex.

Orwell: I . . . oh . . . *Anand looks beautiful in this light.*

Anand: The source of all change . . . Energy . . . the raw source . . .

Orwell: I . . .

Anand: Speak, my friend.

Orwell: I . . . know someday change will come.

Orwell collapses out of the pose and lies on the floor, his face turned away from Anand. He has missed his chance. Anand goes to his room. Orwell goes to kitchen for breakfast. January comes in, sleepy.

Orwell: You know, I think I need to be more in touch with the wisdom of the East.

January: Oh? Great.

Orwell: I'm really learning a lot, being around Anand.

January: I'm sure.

Orwell: I think he could be a guru.

January: I think he thinks so too.

Orwell: Aren't you two getting along?

January: Oh, yeah, but . . .

Orwell: *Anand-like, a rhetorical question.* How to comprehend the ancient life of Eastern cultures?

January: Yeah, if I say something is wrong, he throws some ancient Eastern precedent at me . . . Maybe if, if I learned the stories. Tried to see things from his perspective, then would his arguments make any more sense?

Orwell nods sagely then looks confused. January gets supplies to insulate windows and goes to Anand's room, knocks and enters.

January: I'm doing all the windows, do you mind?

Anand: Not at all, not at all. I will do it.

January: Do you know how?

Anand: When hands are willing, mind will follow.

January starts. Anand may fiddle with the odd sheet.

January: Anand, how did you learn the stories and philosophy, say, the *Mahabharata*? Did you read them, or . . .

Anand: But they are in the air.

January: What's that mean?

Anand: Our great stories, they are taught in schools, sung in festivals, given as examples when children misbehave. They are dramatized as TV serials and the entire country stops to watch.

January: Funny people haven't got bored of them by now.

Anand: The Indian mind does not fear repetition. Innovation, that is the cause for panic.

January starts blowdrying sheet of plastic to shrink it onto window.

Amma and Appa appear to Tamil movie music. They seem to be fighting a wind. January shuts off the blowdryer, and the wind goes away. Amma pats her frazzled hair into place, and Appa belches, while twitching and tucking his dhoti.

Amma: *To Appa.* Tell him. Tell him. *No response.* Anand . . . *Starting to swoon* . . . your own sister, your . . . she is . . . thinking of . . . marrying some no-caste co-worker . . .

Anand: Achcha. What to do?

Amma: You know this is verrry serious! Is my daughter going to perform rituals for the ancestors of untouchables?

Anand: Amma, Lakshmi is one very sensible girl, Amma. No doubt any boy of her choice would be one hard-working, reliable sort.

Amma: Very good, that sort, to marry his own kind.

Anand: And caste barriers are not what they have been.

Amma: No, not what they have been, nothing to stop them . . . everything is changing so . . . ooohh, ooohh. *Overcome.*

Appa: There, there. No need to get worked up. I will send the boy to drive in the water buffaloes, and the rains are coming soon.

Anand: My very dearest Amma, you object to this marriage on grounds of caste. But scriptures say caste is not determined by birth but by merit—

Amma: This is our reward for educating you? Talking such things, eating meat that is not meat . . .

January: Ask them if they've spoken with Lakshmi.

Anand: Have you talked with Lakshmi on this matter?

Amma: She doesn't see us, she doesn't hear us. Not one word! I don't know how to, I can't talk to my daughters these days. Vidya hears everything.

Anand: *To January.* Vidya Aunty keeps abreast of all the news, in this world and the next. She always said she could not act like a proper widow because her husband still visited her all the time.

Amma: You are thinking this girl is the one to bring comfort and warmth into our home?

Anand: January is on the maintenance committee and is installing energy saving devices.

Amma: Why are you not a graduate yet, Anand? How can I talk to people, what can I say? For our conversation and status, you must finish your studies and then marry who we choose. Some nice girl—of our caste. So many worries.

Appa: The only worry you should have is your hubby's performance on the cricket pitch. We beat them at their own game!!

Amma: If Lakshmi . . . Oh, you know the scandal that will rain? Pouring on our heads?

Anand: Too well I know it, Amma. *January pokes him* . . . but it is no one else's business—

Appa: Forget the business for a day! This evening, we will pretend we are people of leisure. We will sit and discourse, and you, my dear, you can bring your embroidery, and the sun will set around us. Don't cry. Life is too short.

Amma: Life is too short, Anand. Listen to your father. Do something. Correct this situation! *They leave abruptly.*

January: *After a pause.* You'll figure out what to do.

Anand: Doing, doing, doing. Can one not just be?

NIGHT

As sun sets, Orwell, on his own in his room, looks around furtively, then assumes the Cobra position, and waits, expectantly. Checks in the mirror to see if he looks any different. At that moment, the blue light flashes. Orwell thinks he sees something in the mirror, but when he looks around, it is not there.

Anand lies awake. Amma and Appa doze in their customary places in his room—Amma snores and Appa mutters.

Anand rises and writes.

Anand: On the plains of war, Arjuna is each and every man. He is awaiting God's okay to open fire on his near and not so dear.

January has fallen asleep in her chair, but the film plays on, with Pentangle's "Once I had a Sweetheart."

The film shows:

—Sara gestures the camera over, she has the documents, the certificate of incorporation which she displays proudly to the camera, then starts to put in a frame.

—Freakette arguing with Freaky. Freaky comes over and makes a rude comment to the camera about how incorporating is selling out, maybe making Nazi salutes, miming a tie, Sara gives him the finger.

January has a nightmare, wakes up, pads over to Anand's room, knocks and opens the door. The film stops when she leaves her room. They move out to the balcony.

January: I wish she could have saved herself, if only for me. I just . . . miss her.

Anand: East and West: your mother is with you, still of this world, and yet she is gone; my parents have gone and yet they are still with me. What to do?

January: All the matters you haven't resolved will only haunt you.

Anand: But nothing is ever really resolved. Come . . . let us soar above these petty contradictions. *Taking her hand.*

January: Why am I scared we might fall?

Leaf gathers up any snakes she has left around the house, takes them to her room.

DAY

Anand and Orwell come in together from outside. Their hair is wet. They carry towels.

Orwell: Banana?

Anand: With pleasure.

Anand gets rid of the towels. Orwell returns with two bananas.

Orwell: Bananas. They, like, rebalance your ions, potassium, and all that.

They eat in companionable silence.

Orwell: Like I said, I swim pretty much every couple of days. Come whenever you want.

Anand: So I shall.

Loud banging on the door. January answers it, wearing an apron, holding a knife and tomato.

Guy: Leaf?

January: *In doorway.* She hasn't left her room since yesterday.

Guy gets around January, runs up to Leaf's door, bangs on it, then knocks softly.

Guy: Leaf! Oh, I love that name. I'm here for you. Run away with me. Let me look after you. Leaf! Leee-eaf. Leaf.

Leaf: *Opens the door.* You're an emotional infant, Guy. I don't need anyone to look after me, much less someone as incapable as you.

Guy: We can be strong for each other. *Seductive.* Remember?

Leaf looks at Guy, there are sparks, she grabs him, they enter her room. January goes back to kitchen.

Orwell: *To Anand.* You're in good shape.

Anand: The body cares for itself.

Orwell: Yeah, you have to listen to your body, listen to what it's telling you, and . . . yeah.

Anand: Your body speaks to you, Orwell?

Orwell: I guess, I just don't think it speaks English . . . I think it's always kind of scared me, having a body. Like my body is separate from me.

Anand: Ah, perhaps you transcend the base needs of this mortal trapping.

Orwell: Um, well, isn't it important, to be in touch with your body?

Anand: O yes, to be in touch with the body, to renounce the body. What is it, after all, but a temporary shell?

Orwell: Oh, exactly . . .

Anand: Be aware of the body, but not attached to the body.

Orwell: Yeah . . .

Anand: In this world but not of this world.

Orwell: Uh-huh, mmm . . .

Leaf's door opens.

Guy: This can never happen again. I'm out of your life, Leaf.

Leaf: Like you were before?

Guy: You're the only woman for me.

Leaf: Bullshit.

Leaf pulls him into a hot, passionate embrace. Guy submits. Orwell is mesmerized. Guy extricates himself.

Guy: We're combustion. Combustib . . . we're setting fires. It's too dangerous. Say good-bye. I'm not coming back.

Leaf: You're right. I don't know what I was thinking. Bye.

Guy: I thought you wanted me to stay.

Leaf: A moment of weakness. I never want to see you again. Bye.

Guy: You can't get rid of me that easily. What we have is too big.

Leaf rolls her eyes and gives Guy one last shove in the direction of the front door. Goes into her room, shutting the door abruptly. DO NOT DISTURB sign is still in place. Guy leaves as January checks the mail.

January: Another letter from Lakshmi. You want me to read you this one, too? *She's opened it by the time she finishes asking.*

"Anand Anna: Where are you? You must not have received my last letter because I know if you had you would have phoned immediately. Ravi and I have to get married, NOW, because Rajan Uncle is contacting prospects. Phone me right away. It is desperate.

Vidya Aunty is still in good health, although she is sleeping about twenty-one hours a day now. She thinks she is taking a short afternoon nap but doesn't wake up until four A.M., in time to do kolam and puja, then a short morning nap which lasts until supper, then she will lie down and not wake until sunset the next day. She keeps a perfect schedule, but refuses to believe she is actually missing two days in three, bless her. She still hears voices, she gets that amused expression on her face.

Uma will probably take top rank in her college class and is still tennis and volleyball captain. She sends her love. Listen to this: she has already told me she wants to make sure her husband is a high achiever from a good family, so she wants an arranged marriage. Who ever thought *I* would be the rebel daughter? Your loving sister, Lakshmi." *January carefully refolds aerogram.* She won't do anything without you . . . At the risk of perpetuating stereotypes, I have to ask: is it your fatalism that's paralysing you?

Anand: You are too, too clever, January. I do not choose my destiny. Nor even my actions. But this does not mean less responsibility. Pre-destination means my responsibilities are still greater.

January: How?

Anand: I must carry out my destined choice. And then I will pay. How do I know if my actions are the right ones?

January: Figure out what you believe in and do something about it. There aren't any absolute wrongs or rights. As you said before, it's relative.

Anand: Right or wrong is relative, but the action is absolute. Once it is done, there is no undoing the consequences.

January: But you're not doing one thing or the other thing. You're only talking and not doing anything at all.

Loud pounding on the door. The doorbell is rung a couple of times, it fails, it is smashed.

January: What the hell? *Opens door.* Guy, what is your problem?

Gui: *Enters.* Leaf!! Leaf!! Where's my boy?

January: Why do you keep insisting you're the father of—

Leaf: *Opens door.* He's not here, Gui. How did you find us?

Gui: He is here.

Leaf: No, he lives here. He's at my parents' right now.

Gui: Getting his mind poisoned against his old man.

Leaf: No, in fact we don't spend all our time talking about you.

Gui: I need to see my son.

Leaf: Where the hell have you been for two years, then?

Gui: I have a right to my son.

Leaf: You gave up your rights when you left.

Gui: The hell I did. I just needed some time. God, I'm sorry, Leaf— for everything. You look great. It's so great to see you again. Still doing the snakes?

Leaf: I'm working on some bigger pieces now.

Gui: Never stopped thinking about you. Not for a second.

January: I'm going to be sick!

Gui: *Indicating the others.* Who are these clowns?

Leaf: They live here. I, I can't deal with this right now, Gui. I need some time to think. Where are you staying?

Gui: Here. Big house. I need time to think too, and to be with you and the kid.

Leaf: I . . . you can't . . . stay here . . . you can't . . .

Gui: Go in your room, think, whatever. I'm going to sit here and wait. This time, I'm not going anywhere. I want you back, Leaf, and I want my boy. My boy.

Leaf retires, dazed. Gui pulls out a flask, wanders around, checks out the premises.

Gui: Nice place. Just the four of you?

January: Yep, absolutely full up.

Gui nods, pulls out a cigarette, snaps the filter off, lights up.

Orwell: Um, it's actually, there's a co-op policy. No smoking in any of the houses.

Gui: It's all right, I'm not staying.

Anand: You have a very spirited son.

Gui: Yeah? *Pleased.* Takes after his old man, I guess.

January: His mother's no wimp.

Gui: Leaf's a she-cat. But she's not keeping me from my son. *Silence.* I'll just wait over here until she's ready to talk.

Anand: Patience. I commend you for possessing such an under-valued virtue as patience, when it can be so easy to get what one wants by bullying.

Gui: I've got plenty of patience. Not much time, mind you, I don't like people wasting my time. But plenty of patience.

Gui sits in front of Leaf's room, swigs from his flask, gets comfortable.

Blackout.

Brian Linds as Orwell (foreground), Damon D'Oliveira as Anand,
Mieko Ouchi as January. Northern Light Theatre, Edmonton.

ACT TWO

Lights up.

Everyone in same positions as when we left them. Gui goes into bathroom.

Orwell: It's like she has some power . . . these two guys, like they're obsessed or something. Why? How?

January: I don't like this.

Orwell: Guess we have to say something.

January: Yeah.

Orwell and Anand are both looking at January expectantly.

January: Meaning, I have to say something.

Orwell: You're the only one she listens to.

January: She might listen to Anand. Might not understand him . . . I suppose we could tell Gui we have a problem with him waltzing in and parking himself in our home.

Orwell: Yeah.

January: How d'you think he'd react?

Guy lets himself in and runs up to Leaf's room.

Guy: Leaf!

Leaf: *From her room.* Not now, Guy.

Guy: *Sniffs the air.* Gui's back. *Everyone looks at him.* He's dangerous, I'm warning you . . . He's plotting to take my woman, isn't he? And my child! Everything I have ever held dear . . . Listen to me, Leaf. Are you listening? Good. I am going to prove myself worthy, of you and my son. Whatever it takes. I am your warrior.

Guy roars. Toilet flushes. Guy cringes, points and mouths, "Is that him?"
They all nod. He takes off.

Anand: We will talk with the chap, talk, simply make our acquaintance with him. We are so frightened of the unknown. Yet the unknown may yield the greatest solace.

January: I would hardly call Gui the great unknown.

Gui emerges from the bathroom, sits in front of Leaf's door and drinks steadily.

Anand: In that best loved of Indian epics, the *Mahabharata,* the famous five Pandava brothers and their mother were in hiding from their evil cousins, who were always trying to kill them. The Pandava brothers would hunt, forage, and beg for alms in villages. Food they brought home would always, always, be shared amongst the family members. Then one day, the third brother, Arjuna, in disguise, joined a competition of skill in arms and won the hand of the princess Draupadi.

He proudly galloped home with his intended, and they burst in on his mother, whose back was to him as she performed the evening prayers. "Look, look what 'alms' I have brought with me!" he exclaimed as a joke, intending to surprise her. His mother, believing it was just another bandicoot slain for supper, said without turning around, "Just make sure you share it with your brothers." Hearing the young princess exclaim with shock, she turned and in an instant perceived her error. "Oh," the good woman stammered, "certainly I hadn't realized, you can't . . ."

But Arjuna would not violate the warrior codes of honour by disobeying her command. Thus it was that the good princess Draupadi married all five Pandava brothers.

Gui: Are you trying to tell me something?

January: Guy was just here. Did you know he's living in the co-op too?

Gui: My little brother?

January: I thought you were identical twins.

Gui: Do we seem identical to you?

January: . . . So, Anand, when the Pandavas go to war against the hundred evil cousins, Krishna is Arjuna's charioteer, and the Bhagavad Gita is the dialogue between Krishna and Arjuna, when Arjuna hesitates to fight, am I right?

Anand: You are most right. Quite astounding, I must say!

January: I've been reading up. Arjuna balks at fighting his own cousins in battle, but Krishna says . . .

Blue light.

Anand: "Whence has this unmanly, heaven-barring and shameful dejection come upon you, O Arjuna? Arise! Conquer the enemies! By Me have all these warriors already been slain. I am the mighty world-destroying Time. You are merely the apparent cause."

January: In other words, it's his duty, his path, to stand up, to follow his obligations. To fight.

Light changes back.

Anand: *Suddenly wary.* This is not untrue, in this case . . .

January: It seems to me that Krishna is saying Arjuna is not responsible for the results of his action, but still, Arjuna has to act. He can't just stand quaking in the midst of battle, afraid to take on his elders and relatives—

Anand: How many thousands of years ago was that written? One's duty is not so clear in this day and age, when all strictures and scriptures are hardly followed.

January: Battles still have to be fought.

Orwell: I got into a battle, once. This really mean girl, she kept calling me names, faggot, other stuff. We were eight. But really, I did it because she always picked on this other really little girl in our class. This girl who was really smart, really little. So I fought this huge, tough girl, right, didn't do too badly either. Then, after that, the little girl wouldn't even make eye contact with me. Totally ignored me. By the next week, she and the mean girl were best friends . . . Then I knew: there was no one in the class who liked me.

Gui: Get. Over it.

Orwell: I am. I was just saying, I have fought.

Gui: It's not easy, man, standing up for what you believe.

Orwell: No. It's not easy.

Appa sits on a cloud somewhere.

Anand comes to his room, writes, stops.

Anand: Arjuna—am I Arjuna? Son of mighty Indra, chief of the gods? My cherished companion, do not ask me to be other than who I am. Yudhishtra, not Arjuna. I have sprung not from the loins of war but of dharma. *Begins writing.* Yudhishtra, perfect not in valour, but in reason. Not action. Thought.

Amma: *Arrives.* He's a boor. A boor! That Rajan! So mad he is making me!

Anand: Yes, Amma.

Amma: Clumsy ox. He is our only hope.

Anand: Yes, Amma.

Amma: Of course he will find a workable boy. I only hope he doesn't scare off the family with his talking-talking-talking.

Anand: Yes, Amma.

Amma: *Spots Appa on his cloud.* If you would tell Vidya . . .

Appa whistles a melancholy tune, then vanishes.

Amma tells her beads while Anand tries to write. She can see the living room, he cannot.

January sorts through a big box of mismatched socks. Orwell watches. Gui lounges nearby.

Orwell: You and Anand are getting pretty close, huh.

January: *Shrugs.* He's slippery, I don't really know what "close" means with him. But I don't really know what it means with anyone.

Orwell: You do so. You have a real way. People like you.

January: Thanks, Orwell.

Orwell: In contrast with me.

January: People like you too.

Orwell: Not Leaf. I should just go. Then everything in the house would be fine.

January: Don't let Leaf get to you. I'd miss you if you left.

Orwell: Yeah?

January: So would Anand.

Orwell: No.

January: Yes.

Gui: *Mutters.* . . . bullshit . . . bullshit.

January: Something you'd like to share with the class? *Gui is silent.* Illuminate our small and petty lives.

Gui rises and walks slowly to her, looks in her eyes a moment, whips out his flask like a magician.

Gui: Illumination! *Finishes contents of flask.* Oops! I'm out. Better get a refill. *Exits.* Barkeep! a round of illumination, for my friends here. *Off.* Bro!

Guy: *Off.* Cad!

January: *Picks up a couple of socks and puts them on her hands like puppets. Makes Gui-like voice.* Do we seem identical to you? *Guy-like.* Leaf! Leaf!

Clash of tools, some doorbell noise. Guy enters with tool belt.

Guy: I'm fixing the doorbell. *To Leaf's door.* Leaf! Every time that bell rings, Leaf, it will ring for you!

January: Are you familiar with maintenance guidelines?

Guy: Forget it, no recycled wiring.

January: This could warrant a special committee meeting. For a doorbell. You want to think about it?

Orwell: If we had a meeting about the doorbell, that would count as committee hours, right?

January: *Shrugs, sighs.*

Guy nods total agreement.

Amma: Anand, all these young people in this house . . .

Anand: Yes?

Amma: They are living like one family. They understand: there is more to life than freedom and romance only.

Anand: If—

Amma: Why must they reject their parents? Or else their parents push them out? Tch.

Anand: You—

Amma: No matter what, Anand, no anything: you are our child. You, Lakshmi, Uma, our precious gems. If you did murder—of course I am here to make sure you do not—but even so, you are still our—*Spies January on her way up.* Oh, this one. Anand, we are watching. We are not always understanding. But we understand some things.

January enters. She smiles at Amma. Amma draws herself up, gives an icy nod, disappears.

January: I just realized, I haven't asked your parents what it's like to be dead. I've always wanted to know, but when they're around, I never think to ask.

Anand: If I asked my mother, "What is death like? The questions of life, are they answered by death?"

January: She would say, "Questions are your problem, Anand, not mine."

* * *NIGHT* * *

Leaf sneaks down to the kitchen. Sound of a snore interrupted as the snorer turns over. Leaf freezes, snoring resumes, she gets a bunch of food, freezes as January walks past without seeing her, gets a snack from the fridge, takes it to her room. Leaf continues to her room.

Anand and Orwell play a computer game.

Anand: You are one very-very fortunate person, to be keeping such a good position, a good job, in these misfortunate times.

Orwell: Yeah . . . Just lucky I guess.

Anand: Oh?

Orwell: I've, worked for the government for a long time.

Anand: Ah.

Orwell: I couldn't have known then, what . . . I'm a card carrying NDP. That card's about as valuable as third world currency—Oh, I'm sorry, I didn't mean, I . . . I wanted to work for the government, and not private industry, but it's all sort of the same thing, these days. But . . . So . . . seniority, and I somehow just managed to stay a step ahead of the layoffs.

Anand: You have made yourself indispensable to your department?

Orwell: I'm NOT, not really, helping, much, with this government's agenda. And I'm not stingy or selfish, even though I know you probably think I am, because of Leaf, and everything. I, I really wouldn't mind giving her a rent cut.

Anand: Why—

Orwell: I would pay for it myself. I would love to have that be the policy, rent forgiveness, or rent subsidies or whatever. But not this proportional rent thing policy. I know it makes me sound like a fascist . . .

Anand: No, no, no, no, no, continue.

Orwell: My problem is the co-op might start attracting only people from the low income end of things—not that there's anything wrong with those people. But we should try to attract people from different situations, so they might understand other people's situations more, and maybe want to help or . . . I don't know what I'm saying.

Anand: You have a vision!

Orwell: I do not.

Anand: My friend, you alone can see a future for this abode, as common meeting ground. You alone can see!

Orwell: What about January?

Anand: Hm?

Orwell: I thought January was the one with the vision, the one in the driver's seat.

Anand: Are you simply a passenger along for the ride?

Orwell: Well, you and January seem to spend so much time talking and everything.

Anand: Talking is easy, my good man.

Orwell: I haven't talked for this long at a stretch to anyone since I moved in here. Well, anyone ever, really.

Anand: I am very proud to be your board of sounding.

Orwell: Me too.

January with flickering of film, snacking. Music, Pentangle's "Once I had a Sweetheart."

The film shows:

—Sara gives Freaky the finger.

—Sara gestures for the camera man to come into the shot. He puts the camera down on a picnic table in the backyard, and gets into the shot. The cameraman is Jorge. Sara and Jorge kiss long and passionately for the camera, someone jogs the table, and Sara catches the camera as it tumbles off the table.

DAY

Gui lies in front of Leaf's door, snoring.

Orwell hesitates, then knocks on her door.

Orwell: Leaf! Leaf! Um, are you okay? *Knocks.* Leaf?

Leaf yanks open her door and holds up the DO NOT DISTURB *sign.*

Leaf: Can you not read?

Orwell: Yeah. I just got worried, because you haven't been out of your room for so long.

Leaf: Well, why don't you put your money where your mouth is, if you care so much? It's easy enough to come knocking and acting like the sensitive, new age guy, but when push comes to shove, you'd just as soon see me out on the street.

January shows up.

Orwell: That's not true!!

January: Leaf, we're all concerned, you have been under a lot of stress, with the job situation, this guy, and Guy—

Leaf: Don't bring my personal life into this!

January: Your "personal life" is in our faces all the time!

Leaf: That is so low. I'm obviously vulnerable and the first thing you all do is gang up on me.

Leaf slams door shut, Gui wakes with a start, sits up slowly, lights a cigarette.

Gui: Pathetic assholes. She's got you wrapped around her little finger.

January: Look, what is your problem? Did we ask for your opinion? Did we invite you to stay here?

Gui has already forgotten them. January stomps off to the living room, Orwell follows. Anand comes in from the kitchen.

January: He's right, you know. It's all emotional blackmail. *To Anand.* A vow of abstinence. She's abstaining from us and the co-op until we all do what she wants.

Orwell: It's kind of tough to plan things, when she's not cooking or doing her chores anymore . . .

January: It's not just a reaction to the rent policy anymore. It's everything. I know she's not that stable right now. We don't want to categorically oust her. But how long? . . . And there's the business end. Leaf couldn't afford to pay rent last month, which was fine: she submitted a written request, and we're set up to allow for people coming up short now and then. But rents were due a week ago and she hasn't paid again and hasn't said anything.

Orwell: She's not eating.

January: She is so.

Orwell: She hasn't put anything in the grocery fund for two weeks.

January: I know she said she's not eating the co-op food. But she is. *Silence.* Anyway, she's broke, we can't let her starve. And money's not the issue. The issue is we're being jerked around. She's mad at the world and her situation. Rightfully. But she can't treat us as if it's our fault.

Orwell: She won't hear it if I tell her.

Pause.

January: Okay, I'll talk to her.

Orwell: When?

January: . . . Now, I guess. No sense in putting it off.

Goes up to her room, trips on the stair.

A knocking on the front door. Orwell goes to answer it. January knocks on Leaf's door. Leaf opens her door.

Courier: I have a delivery for Ms. Lillian Ann Whitehouse.

Orwell: No one by that name lives here.

Leaf: That's me. *Opens envelope, reads.* No way!! Fucking hell!! *Runs to phone, dials long distance number.* You can't have him, Dad, there's no way! You can't do this to me—. . . It is not what's best for him. I'm his mother. No, n—. . . No!

Gui: *Materializes.* Let me talk to him. *Takes phone.*

Leaf: No, Gui, this isn't about you.

They wrestle over phone. Anand leaves.

Gui: It's about my son. *On phone.* Listen, don't you think for a second you're getting my boy. You're going to have to deal with me, old man, and you haven't got a leg to stand on—

Leaf: *Reclaims phone.* He's my son and he's all I've got. No, I am not back together with him, he just showed up here. He's not going to get Junior and neither are you. You're only doing this now because you know I haven't got the money for lawyers to fight you—. . . No, that is not an option, I won't move back there, I can't. No, you—. . . Father? Dad? Shit. *Hangs up phone.*

Gui: I'm going to get my son.

Leaf: You are not.

Gui: I need my boy and he needs me.

Gui takes off. Leaf is beaten and deflated. The others are quiet for a few moments.

Orwell: If it's just lawyers' costs you need, I could help out.

A slight response from Leaf.

January: First thing is you have to get a restraining order on Gui. Get it issued now and tell your father, so he can call the police if Gui tries to take Junior away. I'm sure your dad'll have no hesitation . . .

Orwell: Jeremiah, in Blue Wing, he worked for Legal Aid last summer. We should call him and ask what to do first, what kind of lawyer we need, all that.

Leaf: Thank you. Really. I knew you'd come through for me, like a real family, eh?

Orwell: We'll get through this Leaf, don't worry.

NIGHT

Appa takes off from his spot in Anand's room.

Anand at his desk. Orwell joins him.

Anand: Yudhishtra saw the chance finally to turn the tables. He agreed to participate in a game of dice. Lost—his property; lost—his brothers; lost—himself. Finally, Yudhishtra offered Draupadi. The die was tossed: the wife, too, was lost. She resisted when summoned from the women's quarters by the evil relatives, and was dragged by her hair to the court where the cousin-victors made lewd comments and tried to strip the virtuous woman. Her five strapping husbands stood to one side, paralyzed by their slavery to her captors.

January watches film, drinks glass of wine. Orwell comes to her room, she doesn't hear him over the noise of the projector. He is sleepy, and doesn't realize at first what is going on. Then he watches for a while. Music plays, Pentangle's "Once I had a Sweetheart."

The film shows:

—Sara catches the camera as it tumbles off the table. She films Peace-Freak and Freakette feeding each other.

—cut to incorporation certificate being hung on the wall inside, and everyone except Freaky toasting the co-op with glasses of homebrew and spliffs, though he's imbibing steadily. General party shots and merry-making, some cheap camera tricks.

Orwell: Is that you?

January: *Startled, switches off the projector.* What?

Orwell: I don't remember anyone making that.

January: It's . . . the founding of the co-op.

Orwell: How did you get it?

January: . . . my mother's.

Orwell: How . . . that was your mother?

January: She was one of the founders.

Orwell: Wow . . . Wow!

January: It's not something I know a whole lot about, yet.

Orwell: But it's so great! We should organize an evening or something . . . Your mother could come! It's just what the co-op needs right now, to become a common meeting ground. I have this vision—

January: Orwell, she's really not in a position to talk. She's . . . changed. Withdrawn, you could say, in the years since she was with the co-op—

Orwell: She sacrificed her dream to raise a family, it's a story I've heard so many times—

January: I hope she didn't leave the co-op because of me. I don't think I could handle that.

Orwell: But now you've come back, to carry the torch—

January: I don't know where to begin—

Orwell: Begin with bringing her here and asking her. To talk, tell the stories.

January: I have tried and tried asking her.

Orwell: But—

January: Please . . . It's complicated. I'm trying to figure it out myself, and I'd rather not talk about it, not yet.

Orwell: But—

January: Drop it, all right?

She waits for Orwell to leave. Goes to Anand's room. Anand is awake but Amma and Appa are there sleeping. They go to the balcony.

January: They really can't imagine you would want your privacy, huh?

Anand: They would say, if no one sleeps alone, no one must suffer waking alone.

January: Maybe no one sleeps alone, but I don't see how anyone would get to sleep together either.

Anand: That is the other thing they would say.

January: Amazing it's such an overpopulated country.

Anand: Mm. Yes.

* * * DAY * * *

Orwell eats breakfast. Leaf puts money in grocery fund box, smiles at him, returns snakes from her room to their places all over the house. January enters kitchen, sleepy, opens the fridge and looks in uncomprehendingly. Orwell's still hurt at having had his vision vetoed.

Orwell: All I meant, January, is we need to tell our own stories.

January: Is that going to solve anything?

Orwell: Anand always tells a story, whenever a problem comes up.

January: My point exactly. Anyway, "story" has become such a new age cliché, I don't even want to use it any more. "Storytelling," yech. As if all "stories" are automatically wise and exalted.

Orwell: Well . . .

January: Lots of—*makes quotation marks in the air*—"stories" are just stupid and pointless, right?

Orwell: Then why are you trying to learn Anand's—*makes quotation marks in the air*—"stories"?

January: Touché.

Orwell: Could you explain to me the story of the five guys, uh, warriors or . . . with the one wife, and . . . I think I need to take some notes.

January: Sure. I'll draw you a diagram.

Light shift to suggest time passing. Reading from her notebook.

January: Then tears of frustration and anger spilled from Draupadi's burnished eyes. Her accusations flew against the chest of Yudhishtra, the eldest of her husbands, as she beseeched her husband to exact retribution for the wrongs they had suffered . . .

Leaf goes to the kitchen as Orwell departs for work.

January: You're cooking?

Leaf: I'm preparing. Tomorrow's my scheduled cooking night.

January: I know, but . . . That's great. It's great, you're cooking. And we'll all eat together and everything?

Leaf: That is the way it works, January. This is a co-op, remember?

January: Vaguely. Well, in that case . . . *Leaf waits.* It's Orwell's birthday tomorrow. I was going to bake a cake, but I don't want to get in your way. Have you planned a dessert yet?

Orwell returns from work. Carries pile of law books. Sets up in living room to study them.

Leaf: Well, we don't always, I mean, no one around here knew about my birthday. It was before you moved in.

January: Oh.

Leaf: I was thinking about making a cake anyway.

January: If you wouldn't mind sticking a couple of candles on top . . .

Leaf: Sure, okay, is that it?

January: Yeah. Thanks.

Leaf joins Orwell in living room. She sits beside him.

Leaf: Thanks for the Family Court Services brochure. I think they can advise me. Anyway, it's free.

Orwell: That's great. That's a really good start.

Leaf: Guess I'll go down tomorrow . . . don't need baby-sitting . . .

Orwell: . . . listen to this: *Dempsey v. Dempsey.* An order awarding custody to the father was reconsidered because, quote, "The party with more modest economic resources should not be excluded from equal consideration as the custodial parent." Unquote. I'm pretty sure that means your dad is not a better guardian just because he has more money.

Leaf: That's great, this case is going to be so solid. You know what else? Advocacy work is the career I've been looking for. There must be other women out there in my position, and now that I've been through it—

Orwell: Yep, it'll just be one step at a time.

Leaf: I'll know exactly what they're going through, that's the best qualification. I'm totally grassroots and—

Orwell: Did January come up with anything?

Leaf: Forgot to ask.

Orwell: Does she seem any different to you lately?

Leaf: No . . . maybe. Like how?

Orwell: I don't know. Withdrawn.

Leaf: . . . yeah, now that you mention it.

Orwell: Something between her and Anand, I guess.

Leaf: Are those two together?

Orwell: I can't figure it out.

Leaf: Do we allow relationships between people living in the same house?

Orwell: I never thought of that.

Leaf: We all live here. There might be rules.

Orwell: January has a lot on her mind right now, trying to resolve some issues about her mother. You know.

Leaf: Yeah. Mother stuff. *Contemplates.* Like?

Orwell: Like . . . Did you know that her mother was one of the founders of the co-op?

Leaf: She never said.

Orwell: Yeah. I tried to get January to ask her to come out here. I have this sort of idea, a reunion or something, you know, to get a sense of our roots. Storytelling.

Leaf: An affirmation of our history.

Orwell: Exactly. She was really resistant.

Leaf: We don't need her permission, we can ask her mother ourselves.

Orwell: That's what I thought! We just have to find her. Shouldn't be too hard, right?

* * * NIGHT * * *

January sits watching film, music, once more, Pentangle's "Once I had a Sweetheart."

Anand comes and sits beside her. She doesn't look at him, but speaks to him, while film and music play.

The film shows:

—incorporation certificate being hung inside, on the wall, and everyone except Freaky toasting the co-op with glasses of homebrew and spliffs, though he's imbibing steadily. General party shots and merrymaking, some cheap camera tricks.

—camera looks out one window: Freaky pissing in the bushes or maybe in a beer bottle. Out another window: a fist fight starting between Peace-Freak and the Neighbour. Everyone runs out to help or break it up.

January: This was shot at the co-op's founding. It was with my mother's stuff at home. I saw the home movie, so now I'm here. I had to see it for myself.

Anand: You resemble your mother closely, in face and spirit.

January: I have reason to believe . . . that man . . . was my real father. Not the one I grew up with. A few years ago, my mom was notified of the death of a Jorge Guerra. I had never heard of him. He died and left everything he had, which wasn't much, to me. I read the death notice to her in the home. I remember the clouds cleared from the window as I studied her face, trying to read her reaction. She turned to the wall. Nothing else. No clues. After I got here, I found the incorporation papers. Jorge Guerra was a co-founder of the co-op. The man in the film. And I was born in the same year this place was founded.

Anand: Ah, you are the co-op's gift to them, and the co-op is their gift to you.

January: Founding the co-op, leaving it, leaving Jorge, or him leaving her . . . could have been on account of me or not at all. I still don't know. And I haven't found any evidence of her in the co-op. It's nothing like her dream of communal harmony.

Anand: But is not each of us the manifestation of a divine dream? You are the fulfillment of your mother's dream: perfect, in all your imperfection. The co-op, too. Even in all its imperfection, it reaches such heights.

January: What heights?

Anand: Aa . . . a dog, catching a frisbee! He reaches that height, he simply cannot fly. He is pulled back to plant paws on earth, but is his moment less great?

January: . . . sometimes, I almost wish she were dead. But instead she's suspended, in limbo. It's all so damned unresolved—past, present, future. And I feel such guilt. I keep thinking, is there more I—

Anand: Your mother would have gone the way she did with or without your intervention. You asked, she did not answer. But you have asked.

January: And your parents are dead, but they're still telling you what to do.

Anand: Oh, yes, I have been spared any lingering doubts about their last wishes.

January: I have to learn to live with it . . . even if she's not really gone, she's not coming back to me, Anand.

Anand: Thank god the universe breathes for us. *Blue light slowly rising.* Exhaling light and air, the breath of life passes in and out our mouths, through our thin, thin skin, "the seven wise stars sing to us from the sky."

January: And, if I'm her imperfect dream, what if I go the same way? What if I withdraw, discontinue . . .

Anand: *Kisses her forehead.* I will breathe with you.

Darkness obscures January and Anand. Music changes to Leonard Cohen's "Sisters of Mercy." Film shows Sara and Jorge filming each other in their room, nude or nearly so, soft blue light—candles, and lamps with scarves thrown over them, lots of shadows. Sara introduces the room as "our own little piece of the earth." Jorge props up the camera, gets in front of it to mention that Sara actually paid for it. Sara is displeased, says it's his as much as hers, she paid for both of them, for their future. Jorge says he belongs to her (all of this is without sound). This tickles her very much, they start to make out . . .

On stage: the house is dark, there is just a light from Leaf's room. Leaf's door opens and Guy emerges in work coveralls and tool belt, just as Orwell approaches. Guy steps back to allow Orwell to pass. Leaf closes her door, Orwell glances back, Guy salutes, Orwell sort of waves back, Guy departs.

Amma and Appa appear, abrasive bhajan music.

Amma: Oh, Anand! Anand? Anand!! *January and Anand run from her room to his.* Some hope I have now, I am finally starting to see a light in this long dark tunnel.

Appa: Can you see it, Son?

Anand: I think I see, Appa.

Appa: That glow, my boy, is Saturn.

Anand: Yes, Appa.

Amma: Rajan Uncle has a short list.

Anand: Oh-ho.

Amma: God is great! Even if you do nothing, your sisters will still be provided for. Of course you must not do nothing. But even so, we will have an alliance to a family all can approve. Oh, now we can begin to plan!!

Appa: Take, for example, the Five Year Plans of Pandit Nehru. Why not count each millennium as a year? I said. No harm done, buy some time.

Amma: Buying, arranging . . . so much work to be done! No more ifs and buts! It's about time.

Appa: Yes, it is about time: has the nature of time changed? Is it force or subject? Growing weaker or stronger? We must address the questions, and choose if we are to become modern.

Amma: It will all be very modern: Lakshmi and the boy may even talk, before marriage!

January: Aagh! *Goes out onto balcony.*

Amma: *Intending for January to hear.* Once Lakshmi is settled, Uma will fall into place, like a domino, then Anand, my only son, our pride and joy, you will topple next! . . . I know you will not fall before then.

They vanish.

January: Have you called Lakshmi yet?

Anand: *Goes out to balcony.* She did not pick up the telephone.

January: You actually tried to phone her?

Anand: With those closest to us, sometimes words are unnecessary . . .

January: Anand, for Christ's sake! You're not doing anything for Lakshmi, or yourself. Don't you care, are you too scared, can you not be bothered to even try to do something?

Anand: My dear, sweet January. Our mortal limitations upset you beyond proportion. We are talking of life and death only. Why cry so much?

January appears as Draupadi and Anand as Yudishtra in an ethereal forest. Blue light is part of transformation.

January/Draupadi: Where in your heart can you find peace, O Yudishtra, eldest of my helpless, noble husbands? How does your wrath not blaze, seeing me in such distress?

Anand/Yudishtra: Anger is destruction. It kills the one who should be revered, it reveres the one who should be slain. One who is angry cannot distinguish right from wrong.

January/Draupadi: Then with all your reason and justice, admit there is no greater call than to avenge the wrongs upon me, who cannot act on my own behalf. Why do you so hesitate to take virtuous action?

Anand/Yudishtra: My heart burns because you have been made to suffer, you whom I love more dearly than myself. But O, fair Draupadi, wise men control their wrath for only then can they perceive truth.

January/Draupadi: Truth! The idle one who does nothing, leaving all to chance and destiny, that person lives a tepid and useless life.

Anand/Yudishtra: The one who controls his passions shall attain the eternal. *To the heavens or to himself.* O, let me, through self-control, join with the eternal One!!

January/Draupadi: By deeds do we progress. By deeds are we set free. What is to be destroyed, by anger, or otherwise, must be destroyed. Proud and idle Yudishtra. God gave you anger to will you to act. In discarding your passion, you are simply obeying your own will, though you couch that selfishness in lofty terms. He who acts the renunciant when simply a coward, that one is not favoured by God, nor by me.

January marches to phone, Anand close behind. She stands watching as he dials a lot of numbers. Keep in mind that the sound of the other person's voice is delayed by the speed of sound.

Sometime during the conversation, Orwell starts up a popcorn popper. By the end of the telephone conversation the popcorn is loudly popping. He uses the big blue bowl for the popcorn.

Anand: Hello? Hello? Lakshmi . . . *January indicates she'll be in her room, exits.* Hello? *Pause.* Hello, it's . . . Uhh, one-thirty. No,

morning! Yes! Hello! . . . Yes, indeed, difficult. I know. Mmm . . .
no, I am not studying so much, but I have not yet finished my
studies . . . No, a thesis . . . Yes, I should be writing. Difficult to
tell when, these things . . . Yes, what is happening? Hm . . . mh-
hm . . . achcha . . . huh. This is all quite dire. Oh, please, please
don't cry, my dear Lakshmi.

I do give you my blessings . . . How desperate? . . . Oh, no, I am
sure that will not be necessary . . . Okay, okay, I will telephone to
Rajan Uncle . . . No phone yet!? This will be what, eight years on
the waiting list! Okay, no problem, ask him to call me from the
post office . . . Anytime, anytime. And Uma? . . . Good, good.
Vidya Aunty? . . . *Laughs.* Okay, very good . . . Yes, yes, don't
worry. Don't worry. Okay? Okay. Bye then. Good-bye! Okay, bye!
Yes very good, bye!

Anand hangs up, pauses to reflect on what he has done.

Orwell: Popcorn?

Anand: *Less hearty than usual.* Thank you, no, my good fellow.

Anand goes up to his room.

Anand: *Writes.* Sage Vyasa narrates the Great Story even as it occurs.
Sometimes he himself is in the story—*stops*—perhaps meditating
by a lake. The other characters come for his blessings, his advice.
They choose their path and the story continues and Vyasa continues to narrate it. *Puts down his quill.* I think I am not so much
Yudhishtra. More so Vyasa, perhaps. Perhaps I need not be so
much part of the action as narrating it. After all, I am so rarely
able to take my own advice.

DAY

*Leaf rushes in to living room with cake, decorated with little snakes. Puts
it down, lights candles. Anand comes down, January comes in. Leaf runs
out to get Orwell, and drags him in, and puts her hands over his eyes.*

Orwell: What, what??

Leaf: *Singing.* Happy birthday to you! *January and Anand join in.*
Happy birthday to you! Happy birthday dear Orwell, Happy
birthday to you!

Orwell: Wow.

Leaf: Blow out the candles. Oh, it's too bad Junior can't be here. He loves birthdays and nobody knew about mine, but his is coming up . . .

January: The other wings send their regrets too. They really wanted to come, I guess it's just a bad time.

Orwell: Well, it's great, but—

Leaf: Come on, come on.

Orwell: But—

Leaf: Come on!

Orwell blows out candles, everyone claps etc.

Anand: Wishing you many, many happy returns of the day.

Leaf: You were pretty surprised, huh?

Orwell: Yeah, it's really nice, it's just—

Leaf: Oh, don't mention it.

Orwell: I sort of have, like, it's not my birthday today.

Pause.

Leaf: You liar!

Orwell: I'm not a, I never said I . . .

January: How, where did I hear it was your birthday today?

Orwell: It's next Tuesday.

January: Oh well, then we're not that far off. We'll just have to celebrate it twice.

Leaf: Like hell we will. This is going in the freezer.

January: Leaf!

Leaf: Tuesday is my cooking day and this is going in the freezer until next week. *She takes the cake to the kitchen.* Don't look like that, you would all do the same thing if it were your day to cook. It's only fair.

January: Guess we could go out for dessert.

Leaf: *From kitchen.* I can't afford it!!

January: Right. Sorry.

Everyone sits around uncomfortably.

Orwell: Sorry.

Phone rings, January gets it.

January: Hello. *Pause, realizes.* Hello! You're calling for Anand, right? Please wait, just a second, yes just . . . Anand! Anand! Phone for you! It's India. *Into the receiver.* Yeah, he's coming, he's coming. Hello! Hello? He'll be right with you. Anand! Here he comes.

Anand: Yes, hello. Rajan Uncle, hello, how are you, Uncle? O yes, very fine, thank you. No, Uncle, no formality, just . . . Uhh, six-thirty. Evening! Evening, six-thirty. Yes, morning for you, evening for me . . . yes, Lakshmi has informed to me . . . O yes, it must really be too much work . . . Oh, a very good family is it? Oh? So attached, well . . . Oh, I agree, yes, Lakshmi's happiness and safety must come first. I agree one hundred percent. But . . . So it's quite certain is it? . . . They would approve, no doubt, Uncle, yes. Mm, so both parties have consented? . . . The terms, of course. Yes, you cannot rush those things. *January glares.* All are happy, you say? . . . Yes, so it seems, so it seems. Yes, well of course I will expect to be informed of the date when it is fixed . . . When? . . . Um, it is possible I will be finished by then . . . Oh ho, Uncle, I am well aware of that. You know how difficult it . . . surely, surely I will return for that, my dear sister's only wedding, of course. *A weak laugh.* Okay, Uncle, thank you very much. Yes, of course, no, I won't worry anymore, not at all . . . Okay. Thank you. Tata! Tata, good-bye! Okay, bye! *Hangs up.*

January: *Gasps, throws her hands up, leaves.*

Anand: *To himself.* Om Tat Sat. *Going after her.* January.

Anand sits outside January's closed door.

Anand: "My lord, it is said that any two who take seven steps together are friends forever," the faithful Savitri gently called to Yama, Lord of Death. "I have taken more than seven steps with you. Now you owe me your ears." The Lord of Death continued on his way, carrying the soul he had collected, the life force of Savitri's husband. Still Savitri followed. He spoke, "Go back! Your place is with your husband and his corpse lies in the forest." She rejoined, "I am wedded to his soul, not what has been his body. I have no reason to remain in this world. Why should I not follow him to the next."

Yama was pleased with her courage and steadfastness. "Ask me for something that will hold you to this world." Savitri asked for children. Yama agreed and continued on. Still she waited. He felt her patient eyes on his back as he rode slowly away. Finally, he turned. "What? I have granted your wish. Go back." Her reply echoed against the rocks: "You have granted me children, but how am I to have them as long as my true love is dead?"

Lord Yama smiled. "You have defeated me. Go back to the forest now, clever one. You will find your husband restored to you." Savitri ran and held her ring to her husband's mouth. She filled with joy as she saw the clear jewel clouded by her loved one's living breath. *Waits for a response.* January?

January: *Opens door.* It's not Death or the God of Death that's frustrating me, Anand. It's you. You are frustrating me. I'm ready to give up.

Anand: You are not of a type to give up.

January: I give up. Do whatever you want. *Anand laughs.* What?

Anand: You say you are giving up, but even so you come out and challenge me to reply. *January just looks at him.* You have inherited your mother's spirit of initiative, but not of withdrawal. You need not fear, January, that you will follow her. You still do helplessly, against your will, that which your nature compels you to do.

January: You think it's my dharma to stand here, feeling frustrated?

Anand: Perhaps it is. Perhaps it is my dharma to frustrate you.

Leaf and Orwell in living room, huge stack of law books, pamphlets, notes.

Orwell: Now, what does *King v. Low* prove?

Leaf: I always operate on the understanding that a case doesn't prove any absolute truth, it just sets a precedent that later decisions may follow.

Orwell: I think it's so great you're learning all this stuff, because you can really be informed when you talk to the lawyer and tell him what to go for.

Leaf: I've decided not to go with a lawyer. I'm representing myself.

Orwell: Oh . . . is that a good idea?

Leaf: Orwell, any lawyer is just a middleman or middlewoman. Just one more person between me and my child.

Orwell: The lawyer would be on your side.

Leaf: Not necessarily. We're talking about my child here, in case you've forgotten. No one could know my case as well as I do.

Orwell: We could get recommendations. I—

Leaf: Read my lips. No lawyer. What I need is money to support myself while I prepare for this case. I can't look for a job and fight this thing at the same time. The money that you would have poured into the lawyer, for no return, can be invested in me.

Orwell: Leaf, you're talking about, like, a big risk!

Leaf: You think I'm going to screw up! It's a control thing, all over again. Just because you're paying the bills, you think you can call the shots!

Orwell: No! I'm worried—

Leaf: Just like my father! Men! Get it straight, Orwell. You're not God and you're not telling me what to do. This is my case.

Orwell: I never said—

Leaf: Not yours. And you can't control my life with your money. Jesus! All this false generosity makes me sick! *January enters, Anand visible on periphery.* Just when I thought you might actually want to help, but it's always, always about control. Tied aid, just like every male-dominated multi-national. Well—

January: Leaf. Leaf, please. We know things are rough for you right now.

Leaf: Save it, January. No one cares.

January: We've told you we would help you.

Leaf: Yeah, on your terms.

January: No, on terms we could all work with. There's just been no discussion.

Leaf: Oh, right, everything is my fault.

January: There's no fault . . . Maybe a co-op isn't the best thing for you . . . you don't seem real happy with the set up here, so—

Leaf: What are you saying, January?

January: I'm just saying I, we need to know where you stand, Leaf. We in the house need to know if you're in or out.

Leaf: You're giving me an ultimatum?

January: No, I'm not giving you—

Leaf: Don't jerk me around. Where else am I supposed to go? You people have no heart. You could give two shits what's going to happen to me and my child—

January: That is so unfair! Everyone here has been bending over backwards—

Leaf: You, the benevolent dictator, making all the terms—

January: You've abused us long enough, Leaf. You're only interested in yourself. You think no one else has problems—

Leaf: This is not about you! . . . I never thought it would be possible to feel so alone . . .

January: Shit. Leaf—

Leaf: This is my life!

Leaf shrieks and goes into a frenzy, overturns furniture, throws her snakes all over the house. Orwell huddles in a corner but watches. Leaf finds a pair of scissors and starts stabbing and tearing at one snake, pulls the tail from the mouth, guts it.

January: What are you . . . Stop! Stop it! Your snakes!

Leaf: As if you care! You're not capable!

Leaf continues destruction. Hurts herself with scissors.

January: I am so! I am so.

Leaf: *Goes to throw scissors at her, Orwell grabs them.* Your perfect life!!

January: What the hell! *Leaf hitting herself.* Stop it, Leaf! *Leaf doesn't stop it.* Leaf—

Leaf: Don't tell me what to do!! I'm a fucking grown-up!

January: Leaf, calm down, or, or—

Leaf: Or, what, January? You'll call the cops on me? Get me taken away? What?

January: You're raving and I'm not interested. I want you out of here.

Leaf: *You* want me out? Going to have me committed, like your mother? Maybe you should start a home for crazy ex-co-opers! It's not your decision, who goes and who stays. The co-op is not your personal inheritance, January.

Orwell: January's mother tried to live and create something. You, Leaf, should understand. *Telephone starts ringing.* I'm sorry, January.

Orwell runs up to his room. Leaf stomps out of the house. January is too shaken. Anand has no choice but to answer phone.

Anand: Hello. Lakshmi? Lakshmi? Hello? Hello! Are you . . . Oh, no! How? When? . . . oh no. And . . . hah . . . yes. Chacha Aunty? Amarnath and Jaggan are there, no? . . . Uh-huh . . . Of course, I'll be on the first plane. . . . Why not? . . . Hm, do you really think . . . okay. Okay. You telephone to me tomorrow, I will immediately be ready to come. I may anyway come . . . Okay! All right . . . Yes, a shock, quite a shock . . . Uhh, eight o'clock. Evening . . . So long then, tata. Respects to Vidya Aunty and Chacha Aunty. Tomorrow. Okay. Good bye.

January: What?

Anand: Rajan Uncle was struck by a motor rickshaw as he was leaving the post office. After talking to me.

January: Oh, Jesus, Anand, I'm so sorry. Man. Do . . . you have to go?

Anand: Lakshmi is telling me everything is under control, there is no need for me to come now. I told her she should call me daily, otherwise how will I know when I am needed? But she says it is not necessary now.

January: Times like this it's tough to be so far away.

Anand: I know nothing specific must be done, but it's best at these times just to be at the house of the newly abbreviated family. When my parents died, our house became very full. My sisters and I, we felt the loss keenly, but there were aunts staying in the house, with children, tiny immortals running here and there, so the mornings would not be bleak. Always something to laugh at. On the thirteenth day, we celebrated the passing of the souls. The crowds gradually dispersed and faded, but by the time the last guest left, we were already on a new routine, moving to the rhythm of a house of four instead of in the time of six.

January: You're homesick.

Anand: I would like to fulfill my obligation to make noise in the house of my young cousins. They will be missing their father.

January: Then, you should think about going back. Just a visit, it's not for forever.

Anand: Separation is loss.

January: We could be separated by a much larger earth than this.

Anand: You should come with me. *January shocked at Anand's first non-wishy-washy statement.* In spirit, you can be there in person, leaving some of yourself behind.

January: What, exactly, are you saying?

Orwell comes in, starts cleaning up. All is silent. The film begins to play, in wisps. January gets the film reel. The wisps of film start to run backward or scramble.

January: Looks like a good time to cut the cord. *Hands reel to Orwell, who accepts it like a sacrament.* Good luck, Orwell.

Nadaswaram music begins.

Amma shrieks. January and Anand run to Anand's room. Orwell is startled by their running—he doesn't hear Amma—drops the film, holding an end, so it all unravels into a mess, which he struggles to organize.

Amma: Vidya is just one babbling old fool. And now, we learn she is wealthy! None of us knew this! Deceiving-thieving old . . . She has fixed my—*sob*—daughter's . . . wedding—

Anand: God is great!!

Amma: To that no-caste boy. I have lost my daughter!

Anand: Don't think of losing a daughter. Think of gaining a son.

Amma: You also, Anand? Then, it is over.

Appa: The battle is over, and what has been won? India is far from free.

January: *Imitating Appa, teasing.* It is not freedom you fought for, but democracy.

Appa notices January for the first time.

Amma: It is over for Lakshmi . . . There is still Uma. And then— you. You must do for us after our death. You have fallen in your duties to your sister. Will you also fall in your duties to us?

Anand: Amma, I will certainly do the rites and rituals so that you are comfortable in death, Amma.

Amma: You cannot do those without the wife we choose.

January glares at Anand.

Anand: I will do what I can.

Amma: You will not do what I say?

Anand: I did not say that.

January: You didn't say anything. As always.

Amma: Anand, my son. My only son! Why did I ever send you to abroad? We were too-too greedy like. We thought your chances would be better, our family could be wealthy, modern. But not this modern . . . O, what have I done?

January: Anand just said, what your family is doing is not your fault. We progress. Something must be destroyed—

Amma: We are being destroyed.

January: You're being melodramatic.

Amma: You are telling me to just toss off everything we have done for I don't know how many years? What will I tell to the neighbours?

January: Aunty, come on. You're . . . dead. You don't have neighbours anymore. Death, for you, has actually been very liberating.

Amma: We are set adrift to wander in darkness, alonely.

Anand: Amma! Don't talk that way!! We are still your children. We still love you. This family is not falling apart.

Appa: Maybe not falling. But not exactly flying.

Anand: And we still need you. There is a wedding, Amma, a wedding.

Amma: Register marriage. Not a real wedding.

Anand: Vidya Aunty will sponsor a feast.

Amma: Hmph! Very well to give piles of money and say go, get married, but everyone knows Vidya couldn't put a meal together to save her life.

Anand: I'm sure Lakshmi would like your, I'm sure she needs your advice on menu, on protocol.

Amma: If that cow Vidya doesn't block every advices I am giving—

Anand: No, no, I'm sure Vidya Aunty just wanted to start things up.

Amma: Lakshmi will probably not listen, but she should get one new sari, at least, maybe two . . .

Anand: They will need help choosing saris.

Amma: Poor ChaCha Aunty normally helps with that, but now . . .

Anand: We need you, Amma.

Amma: This family is hopeless. Where is your father? *To Appa.* We must make a move.

Appa: Onward, Christian soldiers. New frontiers.

Amma: We will see you there, I am expecting?

January and Anand look at each other.

January: See you there.

Anand does namaskaram for them. January does too. Amma and Appa disappear. January and Anand high five. There is a change of light, the feeling of time passing.

Anand: So, inevitably, the ending that was meant to be has come to be.

January: It didn't just "come to be" on its own. You could have knuckled under and done what your parents wanted. You stood up to them, that's why—

Anand: Why. Why try to say why? It turned out as it should.

January: I'm not going to concede that no action is always the best course.

Anand: For some, inaction. For others, action. Without one, the world would stand still. Without the other, it is a top, whirling out of control.

January: I wanted things to turn out like this for Lakshmi . . . but then, I felt so guilty when I heard Rajan Uncle died . . . Maybe if I hadn't pushed you . . .

Anand: I too felt badly. But who chose the time when he would call, the route he would take, the risk calculation of the driver? To whose action is the guilt attached? For once, January, rest your conscience. You cannot always be on active duty. While the universe spins into the phase of mystery, you must rest. When it turns once more to the light, then open your eyes.

The sound of fluttering wings is heard. January and Anand duck as Appa lands unsteadily.

Appa: Ahoy!

Anand: Oh, boy.

January: Anand, let's ask.

Anand gives her a quizzical look, she prods him, he consents.

Anand: Appa, do you feel different, being dead? With the mask of life removed, can you see into the centre of being and non-being?

Appa: Does the fish take pleasure in swimming? Does the bird fly for fun? For those who follow their natures, what is the meaning of ambition?

Appa takes off.

January: Sorry. I see what you mean.

Anand: On the contrary, I am astounded. My parents are dead and they are just now beginning to make sense.

OUT OF TIME

The sound of a quill scratching is heard. January and Anand wearing crowns, appear in a chariot, with bows and arrows. Orwell sits alone in the living room, reading a postcard.

January: *In a voice-over.* Dear Orwell: India so far seems a lot like the co-op. Nothing works and nothing changes. Charming and infuriating.

Anand: I fulfilled my duty at my sister's wedding. India changes so fast. Two communities who would not have let their shadows touch in the last generation, all were gathered under one canopy for the sake of bride and groom. Forward and backward—

January: Incredible social progress and increasing poverty—

Anand: Six months and a day from now, we will be where you are now and you will have come to here. We circumambulate the spark of divine life, cannot go too close or it will burn us. All these things we have learned—are we not a wise civilization?

January: Anand still seems to think he'll complete his thesis any day now. Or that's what he tells his relatives, when they ask why he hasn't got a job. In theory, I suppose that's one more thing binding us to the West.

Anand: Are you keeping up with your yoga?

January: And I'm very curious to know how you are getting on with the co-op reunion, to find out what sort of people our revered institution incubated over the years.

Anand: The West holds our hope but the East holds our inspiration.

January: West and East should be seen for what they are now, not what they have been or will be.

Anand: We will meet again when we have overtaken the inevitable turning of the globe, if and when we are ever in the same place at the same time.

January: Gotta fly. Write if you can. Yours aff'ly . . .

There is a glowing blue orb in the charioteer's seat. Anand and January fly. Lights go past them slowly, like headlights of cars going the opposite way at night. There is a jolt and Anand falls off. The motion stops as he remounts, then the lights accelerate and finally stream in a zoom effect, illuminating January and Anand in a supernatural shower of light.

Leaf walks from her room toward the front door carrying a box. Guy follows her, also carrying some things.

Leaf: Tell him not to miss the meeting Wednesday.

Leaf exits. Guy crosses to Orwell, kisses him significantly.

Guy: Don't miss the meeting Wednesday.

Orwell nods. Guy exits. Orwell gets into Cobra position, with a sort of resigned but hopeful expression on his face.

MOM, DAD, I'M LIVING WITH A WHITE GIRL
BY MARTY CHAN

All rights are held by the playwright. Inquiries and requests for permission to produce should be directed to:

Marty Chan
10539-75 Street
Edmonton AB T6A 2Z6
(780) 413-6486

A version of this play was published in *Canadian Mosaic II: 6 Plays*, edited by Aviva Ravel, Simon & Pierre Publishing Co. Ltd., 1996.

A scene from a version of this play was published in *Beyond the Pale*, Playwrights Canada Press, 1996.

The playwright would like to thank Ben Henderson, Annette Loiselle, Jared Matsunaga-Turnbull, Mieko Ouchi, and John Wright for their help in workshopping the final version of this play in September of 1998.

First Performance

Mom, Dad, I'm Living with a White Girl had its premiere at Theatre Passe Muraille in 1995 produced by Cahoots Theatre. The original cast consisted of:

Mark Gee—Arthur Eng

Li Fen Gee—Brenda Kamino

Kim Gee—Paul Lee

Sally Davis—Linda Prystawska

Director—Sally Han

Assistant Director—Pam Eddenden

Choreographer—Xing Bang Fu

Stage Manager—Maria Costa

Producer/Production Manager—Marion de Vries

A second production, directed by Donna Spenser, ran at the Firehall Arts Centre in Vancouver. The cast consisted of John James Hong, Donna Yamamoto, Kirsten Robeck, and Daniel Chen.

Since these productions, major revisions were made to the script. The revised version was presented as part of Workshop West Theatre's Springboards New Play Festival in December 1997. Directed by Ben Henderson, it featured April Banigan, John James Hong, Yung Luu, and Rita Wong.

A full production was produced by Theatre Network at the Roxy Theatre in the fall of 1998. The cast was as follows:

Mark Gee—Jared Matsunaga-Turnbull

Li Fen Gee—Laara Ong

Kim Gee—Patrick Gallagher

Sally Davis—Caroline Livingstone

Director—Ben Henderson

Production Design—Robert Shannon

Fight Choreographer—Paul Gelineau

Stage Manager—Shauna Murphy

Music/Sound Design—Peter Moller

Magic Consultant—Ron Pearson

IAN JACKSON

Laara Ong as Li Fen Gee, Patrick Gallagher as Kim Gee.
Theatre Network, Edmonton.

ACT ONE

The lines between fact and fiction blur. Nightmares intrude upon reality until one cannot be distinguished from the other. Fear dominates reason. This is the twisted world of MARK GEE.

Reflecting his nightmares, the set looks like an evil lair of the Yellow Claw, an Oriental warlord bent on world domination, but it can also function as a home and acupuncture clinic. A torture rack doubles as kitchen table and acupuncture table. There are four imperious chairs around the table, facing each other, two against two.

On the outskirts of the set, a DRUMMER provides all the sound and music. His main instrument is a Chinese gong. He rings it, summoning KIM GEE (45).

Kim comes out with a see-through globe in one hand and a long needle in the other. The globe is painted with the continents of the world. North America faces the audience.

Behind Kim, LI FEN GEE (40) lurks in the shadows, with a cigarette in a long cigarette holder.

Kim: The key is the entry point. Find the right one and we can reach the nerve centre. Strike where they are most vulnerable. Ah. The heart of decadence. Vancouver. Yellow Claw, we will infiltrate their society as a moth chews through silk.

Li Fen: Not infiltrate. The East shall overcome the West.

Kim: Yellow Claw, can't we insinuate ourselves into their world with Dim Sum buffets and Chinese takeout?

Li Fen: No, Kim. Two worlds cannot coincide. We must conquer or submit.

Kim: Ah . . . you are wise as you are evil, mistress.

Li Fen: Nothing can stop me from worldwide domination.

Kim: Nothing.

Li Fen and Kim laugh. Li Fen flicks her cigarette. Kim inserts the needle into the globe.

The globe turns yellow. Smoke billows out—white at first, then it turns yellow. Li Fen exits, laughing. Kim follows.

MARK GEE (20) sneaks on stage. He wears a trenchcoat.

SALLY DAVIS (22) enters in a trenchcoat. She is enveloped by the fog. A figure shrouded in mystery and intrigue.

Sally: The canary flies the coop at midnight.

Mark: The panda devours her cubs.

Sally: The cocoon suffocates the butterfly.

Mark: The young tree has deep roots.

Sally: Agent Banana?

Mark: Snow Princess?

Sally: So you wish to defect from the ranks of the Yellow Claw?

Mark: Yes, I seek independence. The right to speak my mind. And the apathy to say nothing.

Sally: Ah, you wish to be Canadian. Well, there is a price you must pay for this.

Mark: Anything.

Sally: As a servant of the Yellow Claw, you surely must know something of her weaknesses.

Mark: She is an inscrutable villain.

Sally: Agent Banana, you must know of some way to destroy her. For the sake of the Western world.

Mark: There might be a way to hurt her, Snow Princess.

Sally: Yes?

Drummer: Yes, yes, yes.

Sally: How?

Drummer: How, how, how.

Mark kisses Sally full on the lips.

Crash of gong.

Agent Banana and Snow Princess become Mark and Sally. She pulls away.

Sally: Mark, people can see . . .

Mark: So? Who cares, Sally?

Sally: The lady on the park bench. What's got into you tonight?

Mark: I'm high on you.

Sally: You bullshitter. Keep talking.

Mark: I can't get enough of you, Sally. You're like oxygen.

Sally: Then breathe me in. Oh God, did that sound as lame to you as it did to me?

Mark: Yeah. Wanna head to the beach and get some fresh air?

Sally: How about a movie instead? The new Ang Lee is running at the Rialto.

Mark: I hate subtitles.

Sally: Mark, he's a Hollywood director now.

Mark: Let's go. Just for an hour. We can rent a John Woo flick after.

Sally: Not in a million years. Forget the beach, Mark. It's too cold.

Mark: *Pause.* Sally, where do you see us going?

Sally: I was hoping the movies. *Beat.* I thought we were having a good time.

Mark: Am I a boyfriend or a movie buddy?

Sally: There's nothing wrong with just letting things happen.

Mark: It's been a year. I figured there'd be something more by now.

Sally: Like what?

Mark: Something.

Sally: Oh great. Let me know when you figure it out, okay?

Mark: Forget it.

Sally: What's been bugging you lately? Is it the fact that I'm always paying for everything?

Mark: Let's just go to your stupid movie.

Sally: I'm the one who's working. You're not going to pull some kind of macho head trip on me, are you?

Mark: Just drop it, okay?

Sally: What is your big problem?

Mark: I love you.

Sally: *Pause.* Oh.

Mark: Thanks for sharing.

Sally: You don't blurt out something like that in the middle of a fight.

Mark: Believe me, that's not how I planned it.

Sally: I didn't think you felt this way.

Mark: Well, now you know.

Sally: You're serious?

Mark: Sally, I've been with you longer than anyone else. How can you think I'm not?

Sally: Two months ago. Remember? Dinner with my dad?

Mark: Yeah . . . ?

Sally: I cared enough to subject you to my family.

Mark: Uh huh.

Sally: Don't you get it? I showed you mine, but you never showed me yours. Why not?

Crash of gong.

Mark: Snow Princess, we shouldn't have succumbed to our primal desires.

Sally: But Agent Banana, sweet is the fruit that is forbidden.

Mark: Oh . . . Snow Princess, you are my queen.

Sally: My little banana.

Mark: Um, maybe we should drop our code names.

Sally: Call me Sally.

Mark: Mark.

Sally: Ah, a strong name. Like Mark Antony. Successor to Caesar. Ruler of Rome. Consort of Cleopatra.

Mark: Sally. Sally? Sally. . . .

Sally: Your concise passion takes my breath away.

She kisses him. Kim enters.

Kim: Infidel! Betrayer!

Sally: Do you mind?

Mark: Careful! It's the Yellow Claw's henchman. Kim Gee.

Kim: My mistress sends her greetings. Hiya!

Kim holds up a shuriken (throwing star) and throws it with deadly force. Sally grabs her forehead. A shuriken is imbedded there. She turns to Mark.

Sally: Smells like highly concentrated opium. It will knock out an adult in three sec—unh!

She passes out and flops to the ground.

Mark: Snow Princess? Sally? Wake up.

Kim: The price for consorting with the white devil is certain and slow death.

Mark: I would never betray the Yellow Claw.

Kim: Liar. What have you told the infidel?

Mark: Nothing.

Kim: You will talk.

Mark: Never.

Kim: Then you will break like so many Taiwanese toys. Hiya!

Kim hurls the shuriken. Mark ducks. A ricochet sound as the shuriken bounces off the Drummer's gong. The Drummer is caught off guard.

Drummer: Hey! Aim! Fucker!

Kim: So sorry. Hiya!

Kim holds up a shuriken and throws it. Mark clutches his forehead—the shuriken is there. He falls beside Sally.

Crash of gong as Kim backs out.

Mark and Sally sit up.

Sally: Mark, everyone has trouble with their parents.

Mark: Not like mine.

Sally: Do you think my mother and I are soulmates? Hallmark doesn't have enough cards to cover the crap she pulls.

Mark: Trust me, Sally. The less I see of them, the longer they'll live.

Sally: Okay, fine. Whatever. I'm just telling you why I didn't think you were serious.

Mark: I want us to go on, Sally.

Sally: Then introduce me to them. I promise I won't embarrass you.

Mark: It's not you I'm worried about.

Sally: Come on, let me impress them. I'll wow them with my Cantonese.

Mark: Yeah, you'll end up calling my mom a prostitute by mistake.

Sally: My Chinese is good, swo ji (silly boy).

Mark: I told you.

Sally: *Laughs.* Mark . . . just give me a chance.

Mark: Anything else, Sally.

Sally: If you're serious about us, this is it.

Lights crossfade to the table. Mark and Sally watch as Li Fen comes out and sets the table. She does everything with ritual, even when she places the chairs around the table.

A tinkle sound. Mark gets up with Sally. Li Fen sees Mark.

Mark: Hey Mom. Hope we're not late.

Li Fen: Mark. *Sees Sally.* Aiya.

Sally: Hi, Mrs. Gee.

Mark: Mom, this is Sally. Sally, my mom.

Sally: It's a pleasure to meet you, Mrs. Gee.

Li Fen: *To Mark.* Aiya, nay mo waa nay ge pungyow hi gwai leur. (You didn't tell me your friend is a girl.)

Mark: Where's Dad?

Li Fen: Downstairs. In clinic.

Sally: I've been dying to meet you, Mrs. Gee.

Li Fen: Look like we have much to talk about.

Mark: Sally should meet Dad first.

Li Fen: You go get him.

Sally: Yeah, it'll give your mom and me a chance to chat. I'd love to learn more about your culture, Mrs. Gee.

Li Fen: Yes. I want to know more about you too.

Mark: Dad!!!! Dinner's on!!!

Li Fen: Mark. Go down and get him.

Mark: Dad!!!!

Kim enters.

Kim: Aiya, what is so important—Oh . . .

Mark: Dad, this is Sally.

Kim: Hello. Wife, I'm hungry. Hurry up.

Li Fen exits.

Sally: It's great to meet you, Mr. Gee.

Mark: We should have supper. I can't stay long.

Mark hangs up his and Sally's trenchcoats.

Kim: What else is new?

Li Fen enters with three dishes of Chinese food on a tray. She sets them on the table.

Li Fen: Make your dad happy. Stay little longer.

Sally: Mark, I'd like to get to know your parents better.

Li Fen: That be nice.

Kim: Mark, get me some tea.

Mark: What's wrong with your legs?

Li Fen: Aiya, I get it.

Sally: Need a hand, Mrs. Gee?

Mark: She knows her way around the kitchen, Sally.

Sally: I want to help.

Li Fen: You guest. Food ready. You start eating.

Sally: Let me peek over your shoulder then. I'd love to see how you make authentic Chinese tea.

Li Fen: You pour hot water on tea leaves.

Li Fen exits.

Kim: Sit. Eat.

Mark: So. How are you?

Kim: Busy. Everyone looking for acupuncture now.

Sally: If you're swamped, you should get someone to help. You know, I've always had an interest in acupuncture. Maybe I could free up a weekend or two and learn about your job, Mr. Gee.

Kim: Thank you, but better to keep it in family.

Mark: I'm a mechanic, Dad.

Kim: No, you are unemployed.

Awkward silence. Li Fen enters with a teapot.

Li Fen: Tea is ready. Mark, why you not eat?

Mark: We were waiting for you.

Li Fen: Food getting cold. Eat. *To Sally.* You need fork?

Sally: I'm fine with chopsticks, Mrs. Gee. This is quite the feast. Do you always feed Mark so well?

Kim: He always get the best. Whether he deserve it or not.

Li Fen: No more talk. Eat.

Everyone eats. Sally proves to be dexterous with the chopsticks.

Sally: Mmmm, it's delicious. This l'aw bok goh. Ho may doe.

Li Fen: What?

Sally: Ho may doe. It's very good.

Mark: Sally knows Cantonese.

Li Fen: Mark teach you?

Sally: No, I'm taking a few courses. Chinese history. Politics. And language.

Kim: Very good. Smart girl.

Li Fen: Yes . . . you speak good.

Sally: D'aw je.

Mark: She said thank you.

Li Fen: Welcome.

Sally: Mmmm, this dish is wonderful.

Li Fen: Shrimp too dry.

Sally: No, no. They're perfectly moist.

Li Fen: You too kind. Have some more rice.

Sally: No thank you, Mrs. Gee.

Li Fen: No?

Mark: She's a light eater, Mom.

Sally: What did I do wrong?

Crash of gong.

Li Fen: I offer you a share of my humble dinner, and you spurn my invitation of hospitality. How rude.

Mark: She's not rude. She's Canadian.

Kim: Eat the rice.

Li Fen: I am only being a good host.

Sally: You call drugging and dragging us to your den of deception hospitable?

Li Fen: I only wanted the boy, but someone failed to obey me.

Kim: Uh . . . eat the rice.

Sally: Never.

Li Fen: Come now, what possible evil could I be up to?

Sally holds up a grain and sniffs it.

Sally: Aha! Truth serum. Slipped a few almonds in so we wouldn't detect the scent, eh? Too bad you used West Indian instead of Hawaiian.

Kim: Yellow Claw, they refuse to eat from the rice bowl of a thousand truths.

Li Fen: Curses.

Mark: Yellow Claw, you are devious.

Crash of gong.

Kim: Eat some more rice, Sally.

Li Fen: If she full, she full.

Li Fen clears the table lightning fast.

Sally: I'd like some more.

Mark: No, it's okay.

Sally: I want more.

Mark: Mom, she loved dinner. Really.

Sally: Yes, Mrs. Gee. It was fantastic. I loved the presentation. It was so authentic.

Li Fen gives Sally the thousand yard stare.

Kim: You too kind.

Mark: She's one in a million.

Sally: Oh Mark.

Sally grabs Mark's hand. Li Fen sees it. Crash of gong.

Sally: We'll always be together, Agent Banana.

Mark: I'd sell my mother's heart to be with you, Sweet Snow Princess.

Li Fen: Kim, take them to the Chamber of a Thousand Horrors.

Kim: I hear and obey, mistress of evil.

Sally: Let me go!

Mark: Don't hurt her.

Kim: What else would I do in a torture chamber?

Li Fen clears the table and exits as Kim shoves Mark and Sally to the back. They watch in terror as Kim transforms the kitchen table into a torture rack. They scream.

Sally: Noo . . .

Crash of gong.

Sally: —kidding. This is an amazing acupuncture table, eh Mark?

Mark: It's okay.

Kim: Hmph.

Sally: Well, Mr. Gee, I think it looks impressive.

Kim: Brand new. Real imitation leather. Looks good, but doesn't cost as much.

Mark: We should go, Sally.

Kim: Feel the table. Soft. Comfortable. Good, huh?

Mark: Dad, one table is just like another.

Kim: Aiya, what do you know? Sally, guess how much I pay for this.

Sally: One thous—

Kim: Fifteen hundred dollars.

Sally: That's a bargain. Good for you.

Kim: I knew someone would like it.

Sally: Mr. Gee, did you read the *Sun* last week? The university is planning to add acupuncture to its medicine program.

Kim: Hmph, only a foolish man would give away his secrets. Acupuncture is a family art. My family passed down their secret techniques to me. It is a gift. How can anyone treat it with disrespect?

Mark: Looks like you've got a rip in the "real" leather.

Kim: It's small. No one notice.

Mark: Guess that's why you got a deal.

Kim: Try the table, Sally.

Sally: Oh, I don't know . . .

Kim: Go ahead. Maybe someone will learn something. I show you some acupressure, Sally. Okay?

Sally: Alright.

Sally gets on the table.

Kim: *To Mark.* You watch . . .

Crash of gong. Kim pushes her down.

Kim: . . . the infidel scream!

Sally: Do your worst. I can take any torture. Flogging. Burning cigarettes. Even dripping water.

Kim: Dripping water? I like the sound of that.

Mark: Don't give him any more ideas.

Crash of gong as Li Fen enters with a plate of oranges.

Li Fen: Aiya Kim, stop that. She not one of your patients. Come eat dessert. I have oranges. *To Sally.* Orange help clear up your face.

Sally: Thanks . . .

Kim: Eat later . . . *To Sally.* Let me look at your ear. Best way to know what is wrong with body is to look there.

Li Fen: *To Mark.* How long you know Sally?

Mark: A year.

Kim: Mark, see these blood vessels. Stiff legs.

Sally: They do feel kind of sore.

Li Fen: And you friends?

Mark: Yeah. Kinda.

Kim: Mark, pay attention. This bump means she has a pain in neck. Hold still. I get needles.

Sally: Uh . . . Isn't there something else you can do?

Kim: It's acupuncture. There is nothing else.

Kim brings a box of needles to the table. It's a traditional box, ancient-looking, probably handed down many generations. He places it on the table beside Sally and picks up a needle from it.

Li Fen: Mark, what kind of friend is she?

Crash of gong.

Mark: I'll never tell you, Yellow Claw.

Sally: Uh, maybe give her a little hint.

Kim: I will prepare the needle of a Thousand Perforations, Yellow Claw.

Kim pulls on the needle so that it telescopes into one long mother of a needle.

Li Fen: Tell me. What is this spirit you two share?

Mark: Something you'll never understand.

Sally: The merest glance of him warms my icy tundra soul. One look fills my heart with joy. One peek sends me soaring higher than the Royal Rocky Mountains.

Li Fen: Blind her.

Kim: Ah, the irony.

Kim plunges the needle into Sally's eyes. She screams. What the heck would you do?

Sally: Aiiieeeee!

Mark: Stop it. She's done nothing to you.

Li Fen: You do not understand. She is the instrument of torture and you are the victim.

Sally: Aaaahhhh!

Li Fen: You will watch as she crumbles from a mighty Canadian into a whimpering blind girl. This exquisite torture is for you.

Sally: Aiiieeee!!!

Crash of gong.

Kim: Oops. Did I slip? Did it hurt?

Sally: No. Not at all. I'm fine. No problem.

Li Fen: Where you meet your friend, Mark?

Mark: Did you know Sally works in the movies? She reads scripts.

Li Fen: What she do rest of time?

Sally: It's a full-time job, Mrs. Gee.

Li Fen: Maybe she should learn to read faster.

Mark: Mom.

Li Fen: Why you never tell us about your friend?

Mark: *Pause.* Dad, let her off the table.

Kim: You like more acupuncture, yes?

Sally: *To Li Fen.* Actually, I think I've had enough for one night.

Mark: Leave her alone, Dad.

Kim: Time to learn.

Mark: I'm not interested in acupuncture.

Kim: No, you just play.

Li Fen: Not now, Kim.

Kim: Lazy. No good. Never do anything.

Mark: No, I just don't do what you expect me to do.

Kim: Same thing.

Mark: You can't force me to work in the clinic. *Beat.* You know I'm right.

Kim exits, leaving his box on the table.

Mark: Hey, we're not done talking. God, I hate it when he does that.

Li Fen: Your father look out for you.

Mark: Yeah, right.

Sally: We should go.

Mark: Yeah.

Li Fen: I not done talking to your friend.

Sally: I have an early start tomorrow.

Li Fen: She just do reading. What matter when she start?

Sally: Mark, tell your mother, it's been interesting.

Mark: We have to go, Mom.

Li Fen: You stay.

Sally: It was nice to meet you, Mrs. Gee.

Sally holds out her hand to shake Li Fen's hand.

Li Fen: Yes, it nice to—

Crash of gong.

Li Fen grabs Sally's throat.

Li Fen: Kill you! Infidel!

Sally: Mmmfff. Agent Banana! Help!

Li Fen: Die! White devil!

Sally: Agent Banana, what are you waiting for?

Li Fen: He will never turn against his own.

Sally: He's not one of you any more.

Li Fen: You think, infidel?

Mark gives Li Fen a judo chop. Li Fen crumples to the floor.

Sally: Good work, Agent Banana.

Sally wraps her hands around Li Fen's neck.

Sally: Now it ends.

Mark hits Sally with a judo chop. She crumples.

Crash of gong.

Kim walks to the acupuncture table, and opens the acupuncture needle box. He pulls out a needle, and carefully starts to clean it. Behind him, his shadows are cast on the back wall. It is as if the generations of his family are watching over him. He works slowly at first, then more aggressively. Finally, he slams the table in frustration. He recovers, puts his needle in the box, and takes it off.

Mark and Sally enter. They wear their trenchcoats.

Mark: You want me to rub it? *Beat.* Are you cold? Let's get out of the park. I'll give you a massage at my place.

Sally: No, I think you've done enough.

Mark: What did I do?

Sally: It's more what you didn't do.

Mark: I don't know what you're talking about.

Sally: You didn't tell your parents about us.

Mark: You're crazy.

Sally: No, I'm your friend.

Mark: That's just my mom's way of coping with it.

Sally: The truth, Mark. Did you tell your parents we were seeing each other?

Mark: No.

Sally: I knew it.

Mark: It's complicated.

Sally: No, it isn't. You just open your mouth and tell the truth. I thought you were serious about us.

Mark: I am.

Sally: Got a funny way of showing it.

Mark: I love you, Sally.

Sally: Yeah, right. When it's convenient for you.

Mark: What do I have to do to show that I care about you?

Sally: You had your chance.

Crash of gong.

Mark: Snow Princess. You have to believe me. I wish to defeat the Yellow Claw.

Sally: Then why did you strike me when I had a chance to finish her?

Mark: I thought you were her. I need glasses. That's why I'm so squinty.

Sally: Wait a minute. I thought squinting was a genetic flaw of your people. Like bad driving.

Mark: No, that's the Koreans. Damn them.

Sally: You're lying, Agent Banana. Don't give me that inscrutable look. You're protecting the Yellow Claw.

Mark: I'm on the level, Snow Princess. There is only one way to be rid of the Yellow Claw forever.

Sally: How?

Crash of gong.

Mark: Do you want to move in with me?

Sally: Excuse me?

Mark: I think we should live together.

Sally: You're insane.

Mark: It's a good idea.

Sally: Mark, you couldn't even tell your parents about us. You expect me to believe you're ready for this kind of commitment?

Mark: Just because I have a problem with my folks, doesn't mean I have a problem with you. Let's move in together.

Sally: Don't you need your parents' approval?

Mark: I don't care what they think.

Sally: You sure you mean that?

Mark: Yeah.

Sally: Then why are you so worried about what they think about me?

Mark: They're gonna think whatever they think. There's no point in trying to change that. Tonight, I almost lost you because of my family. I won't let that happen again.

Sally: You know what this would mean, don't you?

Mark: I'm not gonna push you, Sally.

Sally: This would be a big step. A real commitment, you know.

Mark: I'm ready for it.

Sally: You really are crazy.

Sally walks away. Mark waits a beat, then follows.

Crash of gong. Kim carries Li Fen in his burly arms. He lays her on the table.

Kim: Sweet taskmaster. Please wake up. If you are dead, what will I do? Who will carry out our plans for world domination?

Li Fen: Oh—Kim Gee.

Kim: Yellow Claw!

Li Fen sits up.

Li Fen: What happened?

Kim: It appears that the infidels have escaped.

Li Fen: How could you let them?

Kim: They were with you last.

Li Fen slaps Kim.

Kim: I mean, I have no excuse for my incompetence.

Li Fen: Where are they now?

Kim: Gone in the labyrinth of a thousand twists . . .

Li Fen: Find them.

Kim: And kill them!

Li Fen slaps Kim again.

Kim: And bring them back?

Li Fen: The boy still has many uses, even if the girl has corrupted him.

Kim: He is gone to us.

Li Fen: But not his seed. He can produce many children, ones that we can raise properly. To be demure, inscrutable and totally subservient to me.

Kim: You are always thinking of the future, my evil empress.

Crash of gong.

Kim wipes the table with a cloth. Across from him, Li Fen picks up the handset of a wall phone. She dials.

Drummer: *Voice over.* This number is not in service. Please check your directory or call zero for assistance. Thank you from B.C. Tel.

Li Fen hangs up.

Kim: Don't worry, he will come back.

Li Fen: Maybe something happen to him.

Kim: His landlady said he moved out.

Li Fen: Why she not know where Mark go?

Kim: He didn't tell her.

Li Fen: I don't think this happen if he had money.

Kim: He has to earn it, Li Fen.

Li Fen: Does it have to be in clinic?

Kim: This is where he belongs.

Li Fen: Maybe it not for him.

Kim: He has no choice.

Li Fen: Why not?

Kim: He is my son.

Li Fen: Maybe we call the police.

Kim: No, it will look bad. What will people think?

Li Fen: We should go look for him.

Kim: No.

Li Fen: You come. I need you show me where to go.

Kim: You should get to know city better, Li Fen. You can't stay in Chinatown all time. I will not be here forever.

Li Fen: You not help me look for him?

Kim: No. We lose face if people know our son has run away.

Li Fen: Mark might be hurt.

Kim: He will be back.

Li Fen: I think we should go look.

Kim: No, wife!

Silence.

Kim: Li Fen, all we can do is wait for him. You know how to do that. You have lots of practice.

Li Fen: I don't know what you talking about.

Kim: I saw you Li Fen. I remember one time I got up early to get ready in clinic. Mark was out very late. And I saw you sitting in living room, waiting for him. You must have been up all night. We do the same thing now. Wait.

Li Fen: He might need us.

Kim: He will call us when he is ready to.

Li Fen: How can you be sure?

Kim: When he runs out of money, he will call.

Li Fen: I go look for him by myself. I don't need you.

Kim: Go. I won't stop you.

Kim exits. Li Fen sits for a beat, worried, alone. Then she summons the courage. She heads off, comes back with a jacket and heads for the front door.

She stops at the door. She looks out. The faint sound of street noises. Li Fen can't go outside. She turns around and heads back into the clinic.

The phone rings. Li Fen rushes to pick up the phone.

Li Fen: Wei? Hello? Who is this? Hello?

She hangs up. She walks off.

Mark enters, with a cordless phone. He dials, but hangs up. He tries again. Sally enters.

Sally: Calling your mistress?

Mark: Yeah, your grandma says hi.

Sally: At least you're keeping it in the family.

Mark: It's the least I can do for you.

Sally: So who were you calling?

Mark: I was just following up my resumés.

Sally: Give it time. Someone will call.

Mark: I hope.

Sally: Maybe the feng shui in the apartment is off. That's why you're not getting calls. Let's move the chairs and adjust your luck.

Mark: You're nutty.

Sally: Come on, Mark.

Mark: Okay.

Mark moves the chairs as per Sally's instructions. He sets three chairs up in a row.

Sally: Start with that one. Yeah over there. Good. Maybe another one. Lift from the knees. Yeah.

Mark: I feel so lucky right now.

Sally: One more. Good. Ah, can you feel it, Mark?

Mark: *Holds his back.* I feel something.

Sally: Something's missing over here. Try that chair.

Mark grabs the fourth chair and sets it opposite the three chairs.

Mark: You know, rubbing a rabbit's foot is a lot easier on the back.

Sally: How else am I supposed to see the crack of your ass?

Mark gives her a look, then plops on the floor.

Mark: You owe me a backrub for all that.

Sally: Your parents into feng shui?

Mark: Yeah, their luck changed when I moved out.

Sally: I should ask them for some advice.

Mark: They'll never tell you.

Sally: Bet I could get it out of them.

Mark: You'd lose.

Sally: What say we have an apartment warming party?

Mark: I don't think I can afford it.

Sally: Pot luck. Doesn't cost us a cent. And we rake in some cool housewarming gifts.

Mark: Now you're talking.

Sally: Great. I figure we invite people with lots of money and good taste. That way we get a bigger haul.

Mark: Invite your boss. She's loaded.

Sally: Have you seen how she's decorated her office?

Mark: Then your mom. Alimony must have been good to her.

Sally: Yeah, but we invite my family, we'd have to balance it off.

Mark: Why?

Sally: Why should I be the only one who suffers?

Mark: Forget the parents.

Sally: Chicken. Why won't you invite your parents? They're probably dying to see our place.

Mark: My mom and dad aren't social people.

Sally: They're probably just shy. It's that whole polite Chinese manners thing. They'll loosen up once they get here. I'll even order some Chinese takeout to make them feel at home.

Mark: It's not worth the effort.

Sally: Even if I get moo shu pork. *Beat.* Seriously, you don't think they'd come?

Mark: Doubt it.

Sally: You know they haven't even called.

Mark: It doesn't matter, Sally.

Sally: They're not having trouble with the idea of us, are they?

Mark: My family is not going to screw us up.

Sally: I'd just like to know if there's something I can do to change their minds.

Mark: No. Nothing. Just drop it.

Sally: Maybe I should have them over for coffee. Let them see how we're doing.

Mark: That's the worst thing you could do.

Sally: Why?

Mark: It just is.

Sally: But they haven't even given us a chance.

Mark: That's their problem. Not ours.

Sally: I'll bet if we just talked to them.

Mark: Just leave them be, okay?!!

Sally: Okay. Okay.

Mark exits. Sally watches him, puzzled.

A soft ring of the gong as Sally transforms into Snow Princess. She skulks around the stage, looking for someone. She steps off stage and hides behind a screen.

Kim Gee enters, sharpening his needle. He hears a noise and turns around. Sally sneaks up behind him, unnoticed.

Kim: The canary flies the coop at midnight.

Sally: The panda devours her cubs.

Kim: The cocoon suffocates the butterfly.

Sally: The young tree has deep roots.

Kim: Snow Princess. I'm the real double agent.

Sally: I knew it. But then what is Agent Banana doing?

Kim: He's playing you. You're cello to his Yo Yo Ma.

Sally: I knew I never should have trusted him. All those Chinese are shifty-eyed.

Kim: Once a minion of the Yellow Claw, always a minion . . . eh?

Sally: Yeah, their kind never changes.

Kim: Ahhhh . . . sooooo. *Chinese accent.* We never change.

Kim advances menacingly.

Sally: What do you mean by—Wait a minute! You're no double agent.

Kim: I've always served the Yellow Claw.

Sally: Is Agent Banana on your side or mine?

Kim: Yes and no.

Sally: You're trying to confuse me.

Kim: No, I'm trying to kill you.

Kim chases Sally. She stops him with a raised hand.

Sally: Maybe we can strike a deal. You don't have to sweat under the oppressive thumb of the Yellow Claw. You can come to Canada. Own your own restaurant. Or even a laundromat. Use your ancient Chinese secrets for good. The sky's the limit.

Kim: Could I become Prime Minister?

Sally: No, but your children could become engineers or accountants.

Kim: Could they become Prime Minister?

Sally: No.

Kim charges after Sally. He catches her.

Sally: Okay, okay, okay. Tell me what you desire and I'll give it to you.

Kim: I desire to hear you scream!

Kim moves on Sally with his hands ready to choke her.

Crash of gong.

Kim examines Sally's ear.

Kim: You come at right time. Stress getting worse. Acupuncture will relieve it.

Sally: I was hoping for acupressure. I'm still a little needle shy.

Kim: I can do that.

Sally: So how's business?

Kim: Always busy.

Sally: Yes, I can imagine. Acupuncture is becoming more and more accepted as real medicine.

Kim: When has it not been?

Sally: I mean in Western society.

Kim: Nice to know West is catching up. You want tea? I get my wife to make some.

Sally: No, that's fine. Just the acupressure. It's my neck that's killing me.

Kim: I take care of it. Lie down.

Sally climbs on the table. Kim gives her a massage.

Sally: Ah, that's great. Sometimes, I wish Mark would follow in your footsteps.

Kim: Make two of us.

Sally: Maybe he'll come around. Never know what he's thinking.

Kim: He very quiet. Never talk much.

Sally: Actually, I can't get him to shut up.

Kim: You talking about my son? I never would believe.

Sally: He's always full of surprises. I never know what to expect. I mean, he's Chinese, but he's not. First date, we went to a Chinese restaurant. I had to order, because he didn't know how to read the menu.

Kim: He never liked to learn. He try to be different all time.

Sally: I kinda like that about him. He's never boring. Frustrating sometimes, but never boring. I like never knowing what to expect.

Kim: You get tired of it soon.

Sally: So have you talked to him?

Kim: You see Mark?

Sally: You haven't?

Kim: We not see him for two weeks now.

Sally: I'm sure he's been busy. Maybe if you called him.

Kim: We don't know where he is.

Sally: What do you mean?

Kim: He moved out of his apartment. He did not say where he go.

Sally: You're serious?

Kim: I think he run away from home.

Sally: That's so irresponsible. How could he do this?

Kim: My son is hard to understand sometimes. When he was younger, he never tell us what he do. He get in trouble, he deal with it himself. He try so hard to show he not need us. He very stubborn.

Sally: And stupid.

Kim: His mother is very worried.

Sally gets off the table.

Sally: He'll turn up sooner or later.

Kim: She just want to know he is okay.

Sally: I'm sure he is.

Kim: If you see him, tell him to call us.

Crash of gong.

Sally: I won't rest until the Yellow Claw is annihilated.

Kim: You will never succeed alone.

Sally: As long as Mark Gee is at my side, I cannot fail.

Kim: Agent Banana will see the error of his ways.

Sally: Mark is a true Canadian now.

Kim: He is an immigrant.

Sally: What other kind of Canadian is there? We will treat him with the dignity that we treat all our immigrants. Even the Native Indians.

Kim: You would not if you knew the truth about him.

Sally: I know about his past.

Kim: Not all of it. Did you know he is the Yellow Claw's heir. He is our son.

Sally: That's impossible.

Kim: Do you think we look alike for no reason?

Sally: You lie.

Kim: Then choose not to believe me. Choose to ignore our straight black hair . . .

Sally: No.

Kim: Our almond-shaped eyes with brown centres . . .

Sally: It can't be . . .

Kim: Our jaundiced skin . . .

Sally: Can it?

Kim: He was sent to subtly infiltrate your ranks like MSG in Chinese food. Gain your trust. Then when the moment is right, he will strike you down like uncooked pork.

Sally: No!

Kim laughs as Sally runs away. He chases after her, laughing all the way.

Crash of gong.

Mark enters, chuckling at a script he is reading. He looks up and sees Sally at the door. She's pissed off.

Mark: Hey this script is pretty funny. "Wrath of the Yellow Claw." You gonna recommend it?

Sally grabs the script from him.

Sally: That's confidential material.

Mark: It was just sitting on the dresser.

Sally: Of all people, you should understand what it means to keep secrets.

Mark: What's wrong?

Sally: My scripts are off limits.

Mark: I'm sorry.

Sally: I don't like people going behind my back.

Mark: I said I'm sorry. Now that I know, I won't touch your scripts. *Pause.* You know, this one's pretty good. I laughed more than a couple of times.

Sally: What do you know about screenplays?

Mark: I know what I like.

Sally: That isn't saying much.

Mark: It's got potential.

Sally: You find Asian stereotypes and racist jokes funny?

Mark: It's a send up.

Sally: It marginalizes the Chinese.

Mark: What?

Sally: It makes everyone think Asians are villains and buffoons. The Chinese are more than that. They're immigrants who've suffered and sacrificed for a better life here. And I don't support any script that degrades their collective experiences.

Mark: When did you become an expert on the Chinese?

Sally: We've outgrown these kinds of stereotypes.

Mark: Seen a Jackie Chan flick lately?

Sally: I'm just saying that writers should never be allowed to make up these offensive caricatures.

Mark: He didn't make them up. I've seen these stereotypes since I was a kid.

Sally: What I mean is this guy shouldn't be writing about Chinese people. He's not Asian and that's misappropriation of voice.

Mark: That's big of you to speak for my people.

Sally: I'm just saying this guy shouldn't be writing about this.

Mark: So what if the writer was Chinese?

Sally: All the more reason not to do this. They should leave these stupid stereotypes behind. It's just going to give racists permission to use these awful jokes themselves.

Mark: I didn't know racists needed permission to be assholes.

Sally: I mean let's not invite discrimination back into our lives.

Mark: Who said it left?

Sally: It's better not to have reminders of it.

Mark: No, it's better to have everything out in the open.

Sally: You're one to talk.

Crash of gong.

Mark: How dare you accuse me of betrayal, Snow Princess. I risked my life to join your side.

Sally: No, you've peeled away your yellow skin and revealed a rotten banana inside.

Mark: I don't know what you're talking about.

Sally: Don't play dumb, Agent Banana. You are the Yellow Claw's heir.

Mark: Where did you get such a crazy idea?

Sally: Kim Gee. Your father!

Mark: *Pause.* Snow Princess . . . that was in the past.

Sally: They are your family.

Mark: I've turned my back on their ways. I've cut my pigtail. I've let my math skills slip. I've torn down all my Bruce Lee posters.

Sally: You can't change who you are.

Mark: Yes I can. How can I show you?

Crash of gong.

Sally: You can start with the truth, Mark. Why didn't you tell your parents about us?

Mark: I was working up to it.

Sally: So you ran away from home and you didn't even have the guts to tell me.

Mark: I'm sorry, Sally.

Sally: Why didn't you tell me?

Mark: I thought I'd tell them before you found out.

Sally: And that's supposed to make me feel better?

Mark: I was just trying to find a way to break it to them.

Sally: It's simple. You just tell them.

Mark: My parents are different.

Sally:	That's crap and you know it. I sucked it up and told my dad and mother.
Mark:	And they took it so well.
Sally:	The world didn't end, did it? Mark, I care about you, but this thing with your parents is getting to be too much. I don't know why you're so scared of them.
Mark:	My mom hasn't heard of couples living together. She comes from an arranged marriage.
Sally:	So?
Mark:	She expects a wedding to come before living together.
Sally:	Times change.
Mark:	My mother doesn't.
Sally:	You haven't given her a chance to.
Mark:	She's really traditional.
Sally:	Yeah, but she's in Canada now. She must have had some inkling that you'd end up with someone like me. I mean why come here if you don't want to be Canadian.
Mark:	Just trust me. She'd never understand us living together.
Sally:	Oh? You know this from experience? So how many girls have you lived with?
Mark:	That's not the point.
Sally:	You're right. The point is that I trusted you enough to let you move in with me. And you broke that trust before you could unpack.
Mark:	I'll make it up to you.
Sally:	Are you ashamed of me?
Mark:	No. I just couldn't figure out how to tell my parents.
Sally:	Mark, everyone gets scared. But grown-ups learn to deal with their fears.
Mark:	I'll tell them. I promise.
Sally:	I've got work to do.

Sally starts to exit.

Mark: I mean it. I'll tell them.

Sally: Yeah, right.

Mark goes after her.

Mark: Sally, I will tell them.

Crash of gong.

Kim blocks off Mark's escape route.

Kim: The infidel has lost trust in your words, betrayer. Because she has heard the truth.

Mark: Now I have no one.

Kim: We welcome you back. The Yellow Claw needs you to complete our plans of world domination.

Mark: You won't take me without a fight.

Kim: So be it.

Mark unleashes a few impressive kata moves, supplying his own sound effects.

Kim: I see you have studied with Shaolin Master Way Wong. Well, here are a few tricks he did not teach you. Crane standing on one leg ready to swoop.

Mark and Kim pose, but never make contact with each other.

Mark: I counter. Tiger with unsheathed claws.

Kim: Mongoose with buck teeth.

Mark: Owl with whiplash.

Kim: Snake with arthritis.

Mark: Dog about to pee. Ouch, cramp!

Kim: You fought well, betrayer. But none have bested me in hand-to-hand combat.

Kim shoves Mark to the table.

Mark: You must tell me. Who was your kung fu master?

Kim: David Carradine. *Pause.* Yellow Claw!

Crash of gong.

Li Fen enters.

Li Fen: Why you call me, Kim? . . . Aiya, Mark. You come home.

Mark: Hey, Mom.

Li Fen: Are you okay? You not in trouble?

Mark: I'm fine.

Li Fen: You sure?

Mark: Yes.

Li Fen: Aiya! So skinny. You need to eat. I make dinner.

Mark: I'm not hungry.

Li Fen: It good you home.

She strokes his head.

Mark: Quit it, Mom.

Kim: Where you go? Your mother was worried.

Mark: Nice to see it didn't affect you any.

Li Fen: Why you not tell us where you move?

Mark: I had some things to work out.

Kim: What could be so important that you could not tell us?

Mark: It's complicated.

Crash of gong.

Li Fen: Do you really believe the white devil's promises to allow you to join the Westerners?

Mark: Yes, Yellow Claw.

Kim: You will always be an outcast there.

Mark: I am an outcast here too.

Li Fen: They see you as a lackey.

Kim: That is the worse fate in the world.

Li Fen glares at Kim.

Kim: For some people. You will never fit in there, betrayer.

Mark: I'm willing to do anything to be in Canada. Even learn their clumsy non-musical language.

Li Fen: Tell me, did the white devil say you could bring your family to the Gold Mountain?

Mark: You know I would never do that.

Kim: You are ashamed of us.

Mark: You're evil.

Li Fen: He has turned from us.

Kim: A small matter that can be rectified.

Kim pulls out a long needle.

Kim: Shall I, Yellow Craw?

Li Fen: I have something better planned. But remain close by. I may need you.

Kim: I will stand here and contemplate the number of angels that can dance on the head of this pin. One, two, three, four, five, six, seven—

Li Fen: Twelve.

Kim: You are infinitely wise, Yellow Craw.

Mark: Claw not craw.

Li Fen: Silence. Now tell me what did you and the white devil have in store for me?

Gong.

Mark: Mom, Dad, there's something I haven't been telling you. It's about me and Sally.

Gong.

Kim: Again with the girl.

Li Fen: His spirit cannot be broken as long as the girl is alive.

Gong.

Mark: We're in love.

Li Fen: Aiya, too young.

Mark: There's more.

Gong.

Li Fen: What is this love?

Kim: A Western concept.

Li Fen: Impractical.

Kim: You are right as always.

Big gong.

Mark: *To drummer.* Stop that!

Drummer: Sorry.

Mark: *To Li Fen.* I didn't tell you where I was living because . . .
Mom, Dad, there's no easy way to say this.

Kim: Then just say it.

Mark: Sally and I are living together.

Drummer: Uh oh.

Ting.

Li Fen: You have committed the ultimate betrayal.

Kim: Now you're really going to get it. Hee, hee, hee.

Li Fen: Kill him.

Kim: Right away—What? Don't we need him for the master plan?

Li Fen: Not any more.

Huge gong.

Mark: Mom, Dad . . . we'd like you to come over to our place
sometime. Here's the address. . . .

He pulls out a piece of paper.

Li Fen: What I do wrong? You not like this before.

Mark: What are you talking about? I haven't changed.

Li Fen: You have no respect for us. You cannot live with her.

Mark: I'm old enough to decide what's best for me.

Kim: Even if it mean you hurt your mother?

Li Fen: Move home, Mark.

Mark: No, Mom. I'm gonna live with Sally.

Li Fen: What kind of son are you?

Mark: One that has his own mind.

Kim: Selfish boy.

Mark: Can't you see this is important?

Li Fen: Go play with your cars and white girls. I don't care.

Mark: What are you saying, Mom?

Li Fen: You not welcome in my house any more. I have no son.

Crash of gong.

Kim: She cared about you. Like a mother panda watches her cubs.

Mark: Yellow Claw, you can't watch me all the time.

Li Fen: Apparently not.

Li Fen pulls out a chopstick from her hair.

Kim: Aiya, not the chopstick of a thousand acids!

Kim shrinks back as Li Fen advances on Mark.

Li Fen: Can you truly fight me, my son?

Mark: I'll do what it takes.

Li Fen: Even kill your own mother?

Mark: We were never close.

Li Fen lunges at Mark. They struggle. Li Fen staggers back with the chopstick in her stomach. She chokes and gags as she backpedals.

Li Fen: But you are yin to my yang. Ping to my pong. We are inseparable.

Mark: I have an adopted mother now, and her name is Canada.

Upon hearing these patriotic words, Li Fen falls on the table and dies, leaving us to wonder what really killed her. The chopstick or her son's rejection.

Kim: How could you kill the Yellow Claw?

Mark: I did what had to be done.

Mark goes offstage. Kim tries to revive Li Fen.

Kim: Mistress of malice? Empress of evil? Yellow Claw?

Mark returns with a funeral cloth.

Mark: Leave her. She is gone to us.

A rhythmic beat of drums. Mark offers the cloth to Kim. Together, they drape Li Fen's corpse with the cloth. The chopstick juts up, tenting the cloth.

Kim: What will I do now? Who will complete our plans?

Mark: Is that all you care about?

Kim: What else is there? Aiya!!!

Kim rips the cloth from the table. Li Fen is gone. Only her dress remains behind.

Mark: What!?

Kim: Mistress?

Kim picks up Li Fen's dress.

Kim: Yellow Claw?

Grains of rice pour out of the sleeve.

Kim: AIIIIEEE!!!

Crash of gong as lights come down.

End of Act One

IAN JACKSON

Jared Matsunaga-Turnbull as Mark Gee. Theatre Network, Edmonton.

Patrick Gallagher as Kim Gee, Caroline Livingstone as Sally Davis.
Theatre Network, Edmonton.

ACT TWO

Lights up. Mark stands centre stage. Sally and Li Fen grip each one of Mark's arms. A grinding sound echoes throughout.

Sally: Get away from him, Yellow Claw!

Li Fen: He is mine, infidel.

Mark: I killed you!

Li Fen: I forgive you.

Sally: Let go of him.

Li Fen: Never.

Mark: You're both hurting me.

Kim appears as a giant shadow on the rice screen.

Kim: That pleasure will be mine. Ha, ha, ha, ha.

Mark: Get away from me. All of you.

Sally: Canada beckons you, Agent Banana.

Li Fen: I open my heart to you, son.

Kim: Accept your place in the scheme of things, minion.

Mark: *Sings.* Oh Canada, true native land, glorious and free . . .

Kim: Nooooo!!!!

Kim's shadow washes out.

The women pull hard. POP! The arms come off Mark.

Mark: AHHHH!

Mark stands between the women without his arms. He gapes in horror.

Sally runs her fingers through the veiny bits of the arm.

Li Fen cradles her arm like a newborn.

Sally: Agent Banana.

Li Fen: My son.

Sally: My lover.

The women look at each other. They advance and beat each other with Mark's "unattached arms." Mark falls on the table in the scuffle.

Li Fen: Stay away from my boy.

Sally: You gave him up.

Li Fen: I want him back.

Sally: He can never be yours.

Li Fen: If I can't have him, no one can.

Sally: Desperate words from a powerless dragon lady.

Li Fen: I brought him into this world, I can take him out.

Li Fen holds "Mark's arm" high over her head with both hands.

Sally: Two can play that game.

Sally imitates Li Fen. Simultaneously, they smash the unattached arms against their own knees, breaking the arms like dry twigs. There is a sickening crunch.

Mark bolts upright screaming. His arms are intact.

Mark: Ahhhh! What an awful nightmare.

Kim pops up from behind the table.

Kim: Your nightmare is only beginning. You will pay for what you did to the Yellow Claw.

Mark: I'd do it again if it meant an end to her evil reign.

Kim: You won't have the chance to do anything ever again.

Sally: *Off stage.* Meow!

Mark: Did you hear that?

Kim: What?

Sally: *Off stage.* Meow. Meow.

Mark: It sounds like a cat.

Kim: Did it get out of the soup pot again?

Kim heads to the exit and looks off stage.

Kim: Here kitty, kitty.

Bonk! Sally strikes Kim on the head. He falls. She drags him off, and then leaps on stage.

Mark: Snow Princess.

Sally: Agent Banana.

She kisses him on the cheek.

Mark: You saved me.

Sally: I heard what you said. I'm sorry I ever doubted you.

Mark: It doesn't matter any more.

Sally: Yes, you've shown your true colours, Agent Banana.

Mark: Yeah, and not a trace of yellow.

Crash of gong.

Sally: Mark, there's still some left.

Mark: Well get it off, Sally.

Sally: Hold on. Hold on.

Sally wipes Mark's face.

Sally: There. Got it.

Mark: You ever think of using less lipstick?

Sally: It's off. It's off.

Mark: Maybe I should wear my jeans.

Sally: It's an interview. You look fine. When you get the job, you can wear whatever.

Mark: I'm gonna blow it.

Sally: You're ready.

Mark: I don't have enough experience.

Sally: You've got tons.

Mark: They're gonna ask for references, and then find out I got fired.

Sally: Tell them what happened.

Mark: They're really gonna hire me after that. Sir, the reason why I was canned was because some jerk thought Chinks can't drive cars, so they probably can't fix them either.

Sally: Then use my name as a reference. I'll be the head of Sally's Service Station and I'll give you a glowing recommendation.

Mark: Yeah, that'll be a big help.

Sally: I'm doing what I can, Mark.

Mark: Just let me handle it. That way nothing can go wrong.

Sally: *Pause.* Sure . . .

Mark: Where are my shoes?

Sally: By the door.

Mark: Goddamn it. Can anything else fuck up today?

Mark heads off.

Sally: It wasn't my fault.

Mark: What?

Sally: You can't blame me for what happened.

Mark comes back with his shoes and puts them on.

Mark: I don't have time to talk about this.

Sally: But you have plenty of time to make me feel like a slug.

Mark: We'll talk about this when I get back, okay?

Sally: You know, it was for the best. Now you can get on with your life.

Mark: What life? I'm two days away from welfare. I'm sponging off

you. And I'm late for the only interview I've had in four
weeks.

Sally: Isn't this what you wanted?

Mark: Yeah, I really planned to be a loser.

Sally: You're not a loser. You're going through what every twenty-
year-old is.

Mark: A screwed up life?

Sally: No, a chance to make it on your own.

Mark: You're kidding, right?

Sally: You think I didn't go through this? You think I just landed
my job? I waited on tables for two years before I got my
break. This isn't any different.

Mark: Yeah, it is. You can call for help.

Sally: So can you.

Mark: How?

Sally: Just ask me.

Pause.

Mark: Sorry. I'm stressed. You know, about the interview.

Sally: I know what it's like, Mark.

Mark: Yeah . . .

Sally: I know you'll do fine. I love you.

*Sally leans in to kiss Mark. He holds up a hand to stop her. She smiles
and walks away.*

Mark exits.

*Kim enters with the globe from the top of the play. He has one chopstick.
He sits at the table.*

Kim: The key is the entry point. Find the right one and we can
reach the nerve centre. Strike where they are most
vulnerable . . . the heart. Yellow Craw . . .

Drummer: Craw . . . craw . . . craw.

Kim gets up, looks around, but sees nothing. He sits down.

Kim: The plans for world domination must continue. Two worlds cannot coincide.

Kim pushes the chopstick into the globe. It pops! Now there is only a rice bowl in Kim's hand.

Kim starts to eat from the bowl with the one chopstick.

Crash of gong.

Kim stops eating.

Kim: Aiya! Wife, I dropped my chopstick. Bring me another one.

Li Fen enters and slaps a chopstick on the table. She sits at the other end of the table.

Kim: Aiya! What is wrong with you?

Li Fen: S'ay h'am ga ch'an. (Bastard)

Kim: I did nothing.

Li Fen: Hmph!

Kim: I did not make him move in with white girl.

Li Fen: This not happen if we stay in China.

Kim: Li Fen, you know we had to leave.

Li Fen: You had to go. I had no choice.

Kim: I couldn't leave you there by yourself.

Li Fen: There I had family. Here I have no one.

Kim: You can find friends.

Li Fen: Where? We never leave the house.

Kim: You can go by yourself.

Li Fen: *Pause.* It better in China.

Kim: No, now you have a better life.

Li Fen: Who say?

Kim: I do. You know I would have to close the business if we stayed in China.

Li Fen: You never asked me if I want to go.

Kim: It was for the best.

Li Fen: You always do what best for you, not anyone else.

Kim: You want Mark to grow up like us?

Li Fen: He be better off than he is now.

Kim: That has nothing to do with us moving here.

Li Fen: In China, I find good Chinese wife for him.

Kim: It is too late for that now.

Li Fen: You never should come here.

Kim: I cannot change anything now.

Li Fen: You mean you not want to.

Kim: What do you expect me to do?

Li Fen: Just what you always do. Nothing.

Kim: Wife. Don't talk to me like that.

The couple face each other. There is a definite distance between them. They exit.

Sally enters.

Mark enters behind her.

Mark: Say hello to the newest mechanic at Al's Auto.

Sally: That's great, Mark. When do you start?

Mark: Next week.

Sally: See? You had nothing to worry about.

Mark: Yeah, I can cover my share of the bills now. They're paying me two hundred more a month than my old place. And there's dental after a year. It's sweet.

Sally: Welcome back to the work force. How about we go out for dinner to celebrate?

Mark: My treat.

Sally: Oo, big spender.

Mark: Just call me deep pockets. In the mood for Chinese?

Sally: Always. Wei, lo yut deep hi.

Mark: Excuse me?

Sally: Wei? Lo yut deep hi? I thought I ordered crab.

Mark: No, you just came on to the waitress. Hai is crab. Hi is a woman's front bottom.

Sally: What?

Mark: Crotch.

Sally: Oh. Hi . . . High . . . Hai.

Mark: Better. Just remember. Down tone. Crab. Up tone. Down there.

Sally: Hey, I know this great place downtown. The Kwong Tung. They make great lo mein noodles. Very authentic. Lots of Chinese atmosphere. The waitresses refuse to speak English. So I can offend them with my Cantonese.

Mark: I was thinking of another place.

Sally: Okay. Where?

Mark: Chez Gee.

Sally: Your parents?

Mark: It'll be great. We'll walk right in and tell them I've got a job. I can't wait to see the look on my dad's face.

Sally: Mark . . . they disowned you. Remember?

Mark: Yeah, but I wanna stick it to my old man.

Sally: Just leave it be, Mark.

Mark: And pass up a chance to wipe the smug grin off his face? No way. It'll be great if you're there too.

Sally: Why?

Mark: Because . . . they'll see we can take care of ourselves.

Sally: I already know that. I don't need to prove it to someone else.

Mark: It's not about that, Sally.

Sally: Then why the visit?

Mark: I don't need to go.

Sally: That's not what I'm getting from you.

Mark: *Beat.* It ended weird. I wanted to be the one to finish it.

Sally: Then go.

Mark: No, it's not important. I've got you. That's all that matters.

Sally: You're sure?

Mark: Yes. I love you.

Crash of gong.

Sally pushes Mark away.

Sally: No time for sentimentality, Agent Banana.

Mark: But we've won! The Yellow Claw is dead.

Sally: Yes, but there is one small detail that must be attended to.

Mark: I told you it doesn't get any bigger than that.

Sally: No, not that. All I need is—

The Drummer throws a pair of coveralls to Sally.

Sally: Thanks.

Drummer: Any time.

Sally: *To Mark.* Put these on.

Mark: Why?

Sally heads off stage.

Sally: You'll see in a moment, Agent Banana.

Mark: What does this have to do with anything?

Sally: It will make our victory complete.

Sally returns with a bowl and a powder puff. She spits in the bowl.

Sally: Lean forward.

Mark leans into Sally. She smears his face with white cream.

Mark: I'm turning white? But how did you—

Sally: That's what happens when long grain rice meets Canadian saliva.

Mark: Are you sure this is necessary?

Sally: You long to be embraced as a Canadian, don't you?

Mark: Well, if you think this is the best way.

Sally: Assimilation is the only way. No longer will you be Mark Gee, minion of the Yellow Claw. Now, you'll be Sven Olafsen, Swedish shoemaker.

Mark: Ja. Ja? Ja!

Sally: Good. Now, find a place to hide and let that set. I'll look for a car to take us out of this evil place.

Mark: Can I drive?

Sally: Yeah right!

Sally and Mark exit.

Mark returns with a dolly and a worklight. Kim enters with a folded cloth and some needles.

Mark goes under the table and hangs the worklight, while Kim works on an invisible patient on top of the table. Mark flicks on the worklight. They look as if they are talking to each other, but the table separates them from any eye contact.

Kim: You have much stress. You are holding much back. We must relieve the pressure points and let energy flow.

Mark: Yeah, here's the problem. Oil pan's got a leak. I'm surprised the engine didn't seize with all the oil it lost.

Kim: You must learn to release anger, fear, sadness. It no good to keep inside you.

Mark: Well, the oil does no good sitting on the ground. It's got to grease the engine. Keeps things moving.

Kim/Mark: Good thing you came in when you did.

A heartbeat sound, beats faster and faster.

Mark: But I got to say, other than the pan, your car's in great shape. You take pretty good care of it.

Kim: Thank you. I proud of my work. If you care about something, you do it right.

Mark: Yeah, I know it's hard when you can't tell a gasket from a distributor cap. You don't want to futz with anything in case you make things worse.

Kim: But in time you get more, how you say, experience.

Mark: I guess I could show you a few things. But to show all the ins and outs, that'd take way too long.

The heartbeat stops. The two men talk to each other, through the table.

Kim: Sometimes, no matter how much you know, you have to trust your heart to know what is wrong and how to fix.

Mark: It'd just be easier if I just did it myself.

Kim: But sometimes your heart fails you. Then, you have to listen to the patient to find out what is wrong.

Mark: You'd have to be some great guy for me to spend my time trying to teach you. And you still might not get it.

Kim: That is a chance you must take. Usually it work out fine.

Mark/Kim: Okay, you're all set.

Mark turns off the worklight and gets up. Mark and Kim make eye contact. For a second, both their shadows are on the back wall. Then the front light fades out, erasing the shadows. Mark exits, with the worklight and dolly. Kim wipes the table.

A hushed ring of the gong.

Mark enters, watches his dad work, then steps to the table.

Mark: Hey, Dad.

Kim: Hmph. You run out of money?

Mark: No, I figured you might like to know that I got a job.

Kim: That pleases me to no end.

Mark: *Pause.* Nice needles. But the ones Lo Chang made were better. Whatever happened to him?

Kim: He bought restaurant.

Mark: Good for him.

Kim: Waste his talent. What is point to turn back on what you do best?

Mark: Maybe the restaurant is his dream.

Kim: He burns noodles. His pork is under-cooked. His dim sum is terrible.

Mark: You eat at his restaurant?

Kim: Yes.

Mark: Why?

Kim: We owe him for all the years he helped us. We never turn our back on people who need us.

Mark: Look, I just wanted to let you guys know that I'm going to be okay. *Pause.* Can you talk to Mom?

Kim: She is upstairs.

Mark: I was hoping you might talk some sense into her first.

Kim: Your mother made it clear how she feels.

Mark: I know she'd see things my way if you talked to her.

Kim: What is point? You don't want to work here.

Mark: We're not talking about the business . . . Oh God, is that why you're on Mom's side.

Kim: You belong in the clinic.

Mark: You were using Mom to get me back here?

Kim: She knows how important the family business is.

Mark: I can't believe you'd stoop this low.

Kim: The clinic is your duty.

Mark: No, it's yours.

Crash of gong.

Kim: Betrayer, you don't understand anything.

Mark: I know I'm sick of this place and it's time to flee.

Kim: There will be no escape this time.

Mark: I can beat you. I know your weakness.

Kim: I have none. Now take your rightful place as the Yellow Claw's successor.

Mark: I thought I'd go into music instead.

Kim: What?

Mark: Not a violinist or a pianist. I thought something more creative.

The Drummer strikes a sour chord on a banjo. Kim and Mark look at him.

Kim: Perish the thought.

Mark: Or how about theatre? Maybe an actor. A director. How about a writer?!

Kim: Stop taunting me with non-traditional career choices.

Crash of gong.

Mark: It's my decision.

Kim: This is not about what you want. Mark, you are the last Gee. You must take over the family business.

Mark: You can't expect me to do everything you tell me, just because I'm your son.

Kim: We are family. We look after each other. My father look after me just like his father look after him. You must do the same thing.

Mark: Did your father expect you to move the business to Canada?

Kim: It was for the best. It would not last in China.

Mark: Doesn't look like it's going to last here either.

Kim: That is your decision.

Mark: I'm happy doing what I'm doing.

Kim: What do you know about happiness? You are too young to know better.

Mark: I know what I want.

Kim: Now. But some day, you will want a family. You will want to give your children the best things, because it makes them happy and that will make you happy. That is most important thing. To have family and be able to take care of them.

Mark: There's more to taking care of a family than making money.

Kim: I spend five years here by myself, save enough money to give you and your mother a better life. I do everything I can to take care of you. That is what family does.

Mark: Where's the room for my plans?

Kim: How can you turn your back on us?

Mark: I know what's important. Having the freedom to make something of my life. If I don't have that, I won't be worth anything.

Kim: If you do not have family you have nothing.

Mark: I was going to tell you the same thing.

Crash of gong.

Kim: Tell me what? What could you possibly say or do to hurt me any more?

Mark: My father never loved me.

Kim picks up a spear from the wall. He stabs at Mark, but can't push it into his son's chest. Mark grabs the spear and holds it to his heart.

Mark: Go ahead. Finish it.

Kim lowers the spear.

Mark turns and exits. Kim puts the spear on the table. He sees the bundled cloth and unfolds to reveal it has the Yellow Claw's dress. He picks it up.

Kim: Cruel, cruel fate. You have taken away my mistress and my future. You are an eagle swooping upon my heart. Clutching it in your talons and squeezing it until it is a dry, lifeless organ. Do not stop. Peck out my eyes. I no longer need them. I have already gazed upon the future. Scratch away my skin for I have felt the supple caress of my mistress' hand as she struck me. Oh soft skin, slap me once more. Reveal your soft hand and point me to the path of conquest. Aiya! All our hopes . . . erased by one who was our own.

Kim pins dress to the back wall.

Kim: Oh, empty dress. You will hang here to remind me of what I could never have. Now my heart is as empty as your sleeve. All I have left is retribution.

Crash of gong.

Sally enters with her laptop. She sets it at the table and grabs a chair. She sits down at the centre of the table.

Sally: While the script delivers some moments of juvenile humour, the offering is light, banal and without substance. Because of its heavy reliance on racial stereotypes, the screenplay may be construed as racist and outmoded for today's politically sensitive viewers. Close the fist on the Yellow Claw. Do not consider this offensive piece for further development. Only a base audience would find this material funny. The ones we are targeting are too sophisticated. They will see this for what it really is. We are better than this script.

Lights down on Sally. She exits.

Lights up on Li Fen. She is alone. She has a piece of paper in her hand.

Figures take shape upstage. Only their forms are visible but not their faces.

Li Fen: Gno h'oi tai gno ji. (I'm going to see my son.)

Voice 1 (Mark): Koe hai been do a? (Where is he?)

Li Fen holds up a piece of paper.

Li Fen: Nay gee do hai been do a? (Do you know where this is?)

Voice 1 (Mark): Ho yeun a. Nay dim yung h'oi? (That's far. How will you get there?)

Li Fen: Gno dup busee. (I'll take the bus.)

Voice 1 (Mark): Nay si m'si gno che nay? (Do you want me to drive you?)

Li Fen: M'si. M'go. (No thanks.)

Li Fen looks at the paper. She is less comfortable, more nervous.

Li Fen: Excuse please. I lost. You know how to get here?

Voice 2 (Sally): You're on the wrong side of the city.

Li Fen: I not understand.

Voice 2 (Sally): It's on other side of the city.

Li Fen: Where?

Voice 2 (Sally): Ask the bus driver.

Now Li Fen is afraid, but tries to put on a brave front.

Li Fen: Excuse me, does this bussee go to here?

Voice 3 (Kim): That's in Kitsilano.

Li Fen: You go there?

Voice 3 (Kim): No.

Li Fen: Which bussee does?

Voice 3 (Kim): I don't know. Check the route map.

Li Fen: What that?

Voice 3 (Kim): Get off here and ask the next driver.

Li Fen: I just want to find this address. Please help.

Voice 3 (Kim): Can't help you. Now are you getting off or not?

Li Fen: Sorry. I not mean to bother you. Sorry.

Li Fen is completely helpless and alone. She walks around, afraid. She ends up at one end of the table. Sally enters.

Li Fen: Hello?

Sally: Mrs. Gee?

Li Fen: Your door was open.

Sally: Yes, I was just heading out.

Li Fen: Mark at home?

Sally: He's at work. He's got a job, Mrs. Gee.

Li Fen: That good.

Sally: Can I get you something? Chinese tea? Hot water on tea leaves, right?

Tense silence. Li Fen surveys the room.

Li Fen: Your apartment nice.

Sally: Thank you.

Li Fen: How many bedrooms?

Sally: One.

Li Fen: Aiya, too small.

Sally: We like it.

Li Fen: It better if you have something bigger.

Sally: We can't afford anything else right now.

Li Fen: I give you money. Get bigger place.

Sally: Thanks, but we can manage on our own.

Li Fen: You know problem with my son? He never know what he really want. When he younger, he want to be teacher. He try to go to school all over Canada. Get away from here. But his marks never good enough. He not very smart.

Sally: He's smart enough to be doing something that makes him happy.

Li Fen: I think he still not sure what he want.

Sally: That's something for him to decide.

Li Fen: My son too young to know.

Sally: That's your opinion.

Li Fen: *Pause.* I tell you something,

Sally: What?

Li Fen: Stay with your own kind.

Sally: Pardon me?

Li Fen: Mark deserve better.

Sally: You don't even know me.

Li Fen: I know your kind. You sit at home when you should be working.

Sally: I am working.

Li Fen: Reading not working.

Sally: Are you for real?

Li Fen: You don't belong with Mark.

Sally: I think he's got a different opinion.

Li Fen: Mark will see you for who you really are.

Sally: His salvation?

Li Fen: His concubine.

Sally: What?

Li Fen: When he sick of having sex with the gwai miu, he will look for real wife.

Sally: I think you had better leave.

Li Fen: You only good for the bed. Nothing else.

Sally: Please leave.

Li Fen: He will get tired of you. Gwai miu.

Sally: Get out! Now!

Li Fen exits.

Crash of gong.

Sally stands alone on stage. A light strikes the Yellow Claw's dress hanging on the wall. Sally turns to see it.

There is the sound of evil laughter off stage. It sounds like Li Fen. Sally looks around. The laughter stops.

Mark enters. His face is no longer white. He has a Chinese finger puzzle hanging off an index finger.

Mark: Snow Princess, I think I found the key to our freedom.

Sally: Don't fiddle with it. It's a trap.

Mark: Nonsense. This must point to the way out. It was hidden in the Yellow Claw's bed.

Sally: No good can come from there.

Mark: I'm positive it's a device to set us free.

Sally: I said don't mess with it.

Mark sticks his other finger in the puzzle. He's trapped!

Mark: Shit!

Sally: It's a Chinese finger puzzle. The only way out is to let go.

Mark: I'm trying. I'm trying.

Sally: Hey! What happened to your face?

Mark: It wore off.

Sally: Just relax and let go.

Mark finally gets free.

Mark: Want to try it?

Sally: You're not serious about getting out of this lair.

Mark: Of course I am.

He pockets the finger puzzle.

Sally: You're stalling.

Mark: Why would I do that? I long to leave just as bad as you.

Sally: Then explain this!

She indicates the Yellow Claw's dress. Mark is shocked to see it.

Crash of gong.

Mark: I can't, Sally. My mom's never done this before.

Sally: Well, she showed her true colours today.

Mark: I can't believe she'd do this.

Sally: She just dismissed me because of the colour of my skin. You have no idea how that feels.

Mark: I think I might.

Sally: No, you're used to it. I'm not.

Mark: Oh yeah, it's my cross to bear.

Sally: It's reverse discrimination.

Mark: Why does it have to be some kind of special discrimination for you?

Sally: It just is.

Mark: It's all the same.

Sally: I guess you're right. Racists come in all colours.

Mark: Look, my mom's probably scared. I can talk to her. Calm her down.

Sally: You can't talk sense into people like that.

Mark: You want her to keep hounding us?

Sally: No.

Mark: Then what can we do? Move?

Sally: Yes, and don't leave a forwarding address.

Mark: That's just stupid.

Sally: I do it and it's stupid. What about when you do it?

Mark: I think the best thing to do is for me to talk to her.

Sally: No, Mark. The best thing to do is turn your back on them. Just like they did to you.

Mark: They have to live with my decisions. They can't keep trashing my life.

Sally: It's not worth it, Mark. Just walk away.

Mark: Sally, I'm not gonna let her get away with cutting you down. You deserve better. You're my girlfriend. *Pause.* We have to talk to her. Together.

Sally: Forget it. I don't plan on going anywhere near that woman.

Mark: It's the only way to get her off our backs.

Sally: Why do you care so much about what they think?

Mark: It's not that. I just don't want you to hold my mother's prejudice against me. Let's finish this.

Crash of gong.

Sally: You've never finished anything in your entire life, Agent Banana. You're just a lazy, opium-smoking, laundry boy of the Yellow Claw. I'll wager you didn't even kill her.

Mark: I did. I swear.

Sally: Prove it.

Mark: Kim Gee! Show yourself.

A deep drum roll. Kim enters with his spear.

Kim: Infidel! Betrayer!

Mark: It ends now. Tell her, Kim. Tell her how I killed your mistress.

Kim: The Yellow Claw is dead.

Mark: See? I told you.

Kim: Just as you soon will be.

Mark: You have no power against me.

Kim: No, but as you have taken away my mistress, I will take away the white devil.

Sally pulls her eyes up, making them nice and slanty.

Sally: *Faux Chinese accent.* Oh no, so sorree. You have wong number. I no white devil. I just like you.

Kim: Why do you whiteys think a simple pull on your eyes can transform you into another race?

Sally: I humble Chinese girl.

Kim: If I did not buy Jonathan Price as Vietnamese, I certainly will not fall for your flimsy disguise.

Sally: I Chinese. My name Anna Chui.

Kim: Gesundheit!

Mark: No more cheap jokes.

Kim: Why not? It is the only thing her kind understands. Stereotypes.

Sally: Hey, I'm Canadian. I'm incapable of such low-brow thinking.

Kim: Mr. Moto.

Sally chuckles.

Kim: Charlie Chan.

Sally guffaws.

Kim: Here kitty, kitty. Time for the soup pot. Here kitty, kitty.

Sally lets loose with a riff of laughter. She stops when she sees no one else is.

Sally: No fair. I wasn't ready.

Kim: You are ready for the grave now, infidel.

Mark: Stand back, Snow Princess.

Kim: Why protect her? You can easily buy another concubine.

Sally: I'm not for sale.

Mark: We love each other.

Kim: Then her death will bring me the greatest of pleasures.

The two men square off in a Chinese standoff. Kim has his spear. Mark has his hands. Long pause, then:

Kim/Mark: Aieeee!!

Kim and Mark charge at each other. Cymbal crashes and percussion sticks beat. It sounds like a Peking Opera. The battle is fierce and fast, a Peking Opera-style fight.

Mark blocks Kim's spear, but gets knocked away. Before Kim can skewer the boy, Sally intercepts him and goes toe to toe with the big man.

Meanwhile, Mark grabs a spear off the wall. Kim is about to stab Sally, when Mark arrives. The two men now fight, equally armed.

Mark spins around, throwing kicks and jabbing his spear at Kim, who launches a series of counterattacks.

The music builds to a crescendo as the two clash in the middle of the stage.

Suddenly the music stops. A light strikes the dress hanging on the wall.

Kim and Mark backpedal. A slow click echoes their steps.

The cloth on the table rises up, up, up. A flash! The cloth forms a human figure standing on top of the table. A hand reaches out from under the cloth and pulls it off.

It is Li Fen!

Kim and Mark drop their spears.

Mark: It's impossible.

Kim: It's glorious.

Sally: It can't be.

Mark: She's alive.

Kim: *To Li Fen.* Can it be you? Are my eyes deceiving me? How can I truly know it is you?

Li Fen slaps Kim.

Kim: My sweet villainous mistress.

Mark: But I saw you dissolve into rice.

Li Fen: I am not without my resources.

Sally: You are a woman of many mysteries, Yellow Claw.

Crash of gong.

Li Fen: That is why she does not understand our family.

Mark: Christ, I don't even understand you sometimes.

Li Fen: The gwai lo is not like us.

Sally: Who says I want to be like you?

Kim: A good wife accepts her husband's ways.

Li Fen: She not his wife.

Sally: And this isn't the Stone Age. God, why did I come here?

Mark: We're not getting married.

Li Fen: I don't care what you do with that gwai lo.

Sally: Then why did you tell me to get out of Mark's life?

Kim: She never do that.

Mark: She came to our place.

Kim: My wife never leave Chinatown by herself.

Sally: Well she did this time.

Li Fen: Gwai lo no good for Mark.

Sally: I have a name and it's not white devil.

Li Fen: You come home, Mark. I look after you.

Kim: Listen to your mother. You have to be with your family.

Mark: This isn't China. I don't have to do anything you say.

Li Fen: Stay home. Out there is no good.

Sally: You can't have it both ways. You came to Canada, you have to take what it gives you. Just like Mark and me.

Crash of gong.

Mark: Yes, I reject my Yellow skin and embrace the White world.

Sally: And we will welcome you with open arms.

Kim: She will take away your culture.

Sally: No, we will sanitize his quaint customs and add them to our multicultural mosaic.

Mark: See how generous they are.

Sally: We'll take egg rolls and fortune cookies. Maybe a dragon dance. But not communism unless it comes with Mao jackets.

Li Fen: She is erasing your identity.

Sally: Only the yellow bits.

Kim: The boy was raised to take over for the Yellow Claw.

Mark: I don't want anything to do with you.

Kim: You have no choice in the matter.

Crash of gong.

Sally: Why are you people so close-minded?

Li Fen: You take my son away.

Sally: Mark is free to do whatever he chooses.

Mark: *To Kim.* And it has nothing to do with you.

Kim: You belong here.

Li Fen: Don't say that, Kim.

Kim: Be quiet, wife.

Mark: That's what you expect ME to do, isn't it? Be quiet. Be a good son. Support you for the rest of your lives.

Crash of gong.

Kim: Accept your destiny.

Mark: Accept my choices.

Crash of gong.

Kim: Selfish boy. You never understand what we do for you.

Li Fen: Kim—

Mark: I never asked you for anything.

Kim: You didn't have to ask.

Mark: I don't need you. I've got Sally.

Sally: Mark is old enough to look after himself.

Li Fen: Aiya, she no good for you.

Kim: She can't look after you.

Sally: I don't have to.

Kim: You take him away from what he is meant to do.

Mark: Don't talk to her like that.

Kim: What do you see in her?

Mark: She's my way out of here.

Crash of gong.

Mark: Snow Princess is my passport to North America. Once I'm there I can become a swinging bachelor man.

Sally steps up to Mark.

Sally: Hey! What about us?

Crash of gong.

Mark: I didn't mean it that way.

Sally: I'm a way out?

Mark: Sally, you're more than that.

Kim: No, you are just someone else he can use.

Mark: Stay out of this.

Kim: He will find another one when he is tired of you.

Sally: You were using me?

Mark: It's not like that. Sally, you're the only one who's ever really mattered to me.

Sally: I wish I could believe you. But the fact that we're having this talk in your parents' home makes it hard for me to trust you.

Mark: We don't need to be here.

Sally: They'll always be in your life.

Mark: *Pause.* Not if it means I lose you. Let's get out of here.

Li Fen: Mark. Stay. I need you.

Mark: I've tried to get you to accept what I do. But you guys are never happy.

Kim: Let him leave, he will be back.

Li Fen: You be quiet.

Kim: When he run out of money, he will come home.

Mark: Come on, Sally.

Kim: Maybe I won't be so willing to help next time.

Li Fen: No more!!

Sally: Let's go, Mark.

Sally moves off, but Mark stays put. He looks at his parents.

Kim: Li Fen?

Li Fen: I not lose my son.

Kim: He is turning his back on us.

Li Fen: No, he turn his back on your clinic.

Kim: It is time for him to accept his duty.

Li Fen: Just because he your son, you think he can do what you want. Just like you treat me.

Kim: Li Fen, I never make you do anything.

Li Fen: I your wife, but I have no say. You make me come to this strange place. You say you only want one child, I give him to you. I do everything for you.

Kim: Li Fen, we both give up everything to give Mark a better life.

Li Fen: You still have your clinic. All I have is Mark. Now you want me to give him up too? You never care about your family.

Kim: You don't know what you're talking about.

Li Fen: After everything your family do, you never go back to see them.

Kim: Li Fen, I wanted to go back as much as you did. But we had to save money so Mark have no worries when we are gone.

Sally: Come on, Mark.

Mark: You were using me as an excuse to get away from your own family?

Kim: No.

Mark: Then why didn't you see your parents? Why didn't you bring them here?

Sally: Mark.

Li Fen: Tell him, Kim. Tell him truth.

Kim: Not now, wife.

Li Fen: They did not think Canada was place to go. They want to stay in China.

Mark: *To Kim.* But you still went? You mean you used them and then you abandoned them.

Kim: That is you, not me. It is your choice to abandon us.

Sally: No, it's his choice to grow up and live his own life.

Kim: His life is our life.

Li Fen: Shut up!!! *Beat.* You talk, but you never listen. That is why you are losing your son.

Li Fen turns to her son.

Li Fen: Mark . . . You can go. Do what you want, but don't leave me alone. You are all I have.

Crash of gong.

Sally: This is your only chance to be free.

Sally picks up the spear and hands it to Mark.

Sally: Do it. Now!

Li Fen: You will always be my son.

Sally: Kill her!

Mark looks at the spear, then at his mother. He drops the spear.

Sally: Pick it up. Otherwise, she wins.

Crash of gong.

Mark: I can't do it, Sally. I can't go yet.

Sally: Mark, it's just a part of her game. Christ, you people are supposed to put family above all else. But all you do is find ways to hurt each other.

Li Fen: Mark, no matter what you do, I will care for you. Not because I have to. But because I want to.

Sally: You expect Mark to fall for that song and dance.

Li Fen: I not want to lose my son.

Mark: Who says you're going to lose anyone?

Sally: Mark?

Mark: Didn't you hear her, Sally?

Sally: Yeah, it's the same crap she's been saying since I met her. It's just part of her twisted game.

Mark: She stood up to my dad.

Sally: It's called a fight. It's what grown-ups do.

Mark: You don't understand what's going on.

Sally: No, I understand exactly what's going on. You're caving in to them. Next thing you know, you'll be back home eating Mommy's dinner and working in Daddy's clinic.

Mark: I just want to work things out with them.

Sally: Can't you see what they're up to?

Mark: Yes. I can.

Sally: Okay, fine. Whatever. As far as I'm concerned, you can be her perfect Chinese son.

Mark: Sally, I love you.

Sally: Yeah, I'm a great trophy.

Mark: I want you in my life. But can't there be room for my family?

Gong crashes.

Sally: No, the only way to be embraced in the West is to turn your back on the East.

Mark: You want me to accept your world on your terms. You leave me no space for my own identity.

Sally: Mark, you must shed your past if you want to come to Canada.

Mark: Then I choose not to go.

Li Fen: You can leave, infidel. We will not stand in your way. We have what we want.

Sally: You don't have to submit to her will.

Mark: I am exerting my own will.

Sally: This isn't supposed to be how it ends. The West is supposed to defeat the East. The girl is supposed to go off with the boy. The heroes have to win.

Mark: Aren't there any other endings?

Sally: Why would you want anything else?

Mark: I'm sorry, but I do.

Sally: I feel so sorry for you . . .

Crash of gong.

Mark: I'm sorry too, Sally.

Sally: I'll expect your stuff to be out of the apartment by the end of the week.

Mark: Sally . . .

Sally: The end of the week.

Sally exits.

Kim: You come home. It better for you.

Mark: I'm not coming home, Dad.

Kim: But you said—

Mark: I said I respect your sacrifices. It doesn't mean I'm going to take over where you left off.

Kim: You need us.

Mark: Just because I'm doing my own thing, doesn't mean I've forgotten what you've done for me. Just let me show my appreciation my own way.

Kim: After all this, you learn nothing.

Mark: Didn't you hear anything I said?

Kim: You have nothing good to say.

Kim exits.

Li Fen: Mark, your father, he is set in his ways.

Mark: Yeah. I guess some people can't change.

Li Fen: Very hard to change. Only when it very important.

Mark: *Pause.* Mom. When I find my new place, I was hoping you could come over and help me set up.

Li Fen: You need my help?

Mark: No. I want it.

Li Fen: You can take care of yourself.

Mark and Li Fen share a look.

Crash of gong.

Mark looks to where Sally left.

Slowly, Mark's shadows form on the back wall. He does not notice them.

Mark: The panda lets go of her cubs.

Mark looks to where Kim left.

Mark: The butterfly climbs out of its cocoon.

Mark finally notices his shadows on the back wall. He turns around and looks to Li Fen.

Then he looks out.

Mark: The young tree has deep roots.

Crash of gong.

Lights down

ELEPHANT WAKE

BY JONATHAN CHRISTENSON
AND JOEY TREMBLAY

Catalyst Theatre
8529-103 Street
Edmonton, Alberta
Canada, T6E 6P3

Elephant Wake was written with assistance from The Explorations Programme of the Canada Council

FIRST PERFORMANCE

Elephant Wake was premiered on 19 August 1995 at the Edmonton Fringe Theatre Festival. It was directed and designed by Jonathan Christenson with Joey Tremblay as Jean Claude. The stage manager was Siân Williams.

A revised version of the play had its premiere at Catalyst Theatre on 12 December 1996 with Joey Tremblay as Jean Claude. The director was Jonathan Christenson. The designer was Bretta Gerecke.

Joey Tremblay as Jean Claude. Catalyst Theatre, Edmonton.

There are two large boxes in the USR and USL corners of the stage with a waist-high ledge between them. Everything on stage is covered in papier mâché.

The sound of an elephant is heard. Jean Claude emerges from behind the ledge wearing an elephant nose.

You know a long time ago there, before uh . . . well I don't know what before. But before Jesus and Noah and all that there. Well before even the bible. Well fuck! You know what I mean. That long ago there. It's true that elephants, they could fly. And I don't mean like a cartoon, like Dumbo or something stupid like that. Not with their ears like this there.

He flaps his arms frantically.

But they could float, like a balloon, like this:

He demonstrates.

And I'm not shitting you. This is true. And I believe this because I read this in a book. You might laugh at me and think I'm some kind of crazy guy. But I believe that as much as I believe that Jesus could walk on water, or make water like wine, or even rose up from the dead. So maybe I'm crazy but there you go.

He removes the elephant nose and makes the sound of a car passing by.

I like to lie in the ditch at night and watch those cars go by. They don't see me. I hide in the long grass in the ditch and I watch them go by. And the dust, it flies all over like a big black cloud there in the sky. And me, I'm not on the ground no more. I'm in the sky floating like the elephants did a long time ago.

He trumpets like an elephant and slowly disappears from view, hiding behind the ledge.

Did you know, my name is Jean Claude. A lot of guys, they call me J.C. The guys from Welby, they call me that. I don't mind J.C. That's not so bad. But sometime when they joke there, or bug me to be so funny, do you know what they call me? Do you know what they say? Never mind. That's what.

All my uncles, my aunts, my cousins, do you know what they call me? They call me Chou-gras.

He shows the audience a potted chou-gras.

The Weed. It was pepère called me that. He told me, "You're just like a chou-gras beside the road. Nobody wants you in the garden, they always pull you out. But when they see you there in the ditch they all say, 'Voyons. C'est beau ça.'" That's beautiful. So that's why they all call me that.

He places the chou-gras DSC.

Did you know, me, I'm the son of the twelve of two twelves. Don't call me twelve-pack.

He picks up a twenty-four pack of beer bottles, all papier mâchéd. During the following he sets down one bottle for each member of the family, creating a line that begins DSL and ends DSC.

Mon oncle Eli—Ma tante Lucille—Ma tante Marianne—Mon oncle Joseph—Yves—Yvette—Claude—Claudette—Bernard—Bernadette—Paulemille—Marthe . . . that's my memère. She was only four foot ten. But when she wore her big boot she was four twelve.

He now moves DSR and continues to set down one bottle for each member of the family, creating a line that begins DSR and ends DSC, where it meets the first half of the line.

Ma tante Colombe—Ma tante Florida—Ma tante Rosaline—Ma tante Maria—Thérèse—Sylvia—Jean—Gisèlle—Juliette—Jacqueline—Jacinthe—Leo . . . that's my pepère. He met my memère at a dance and they got married in the Ste. Vierge church.

But before they did Père Champagne, he looked them straight in the eye and he said, "Don't forget: French people should have a lot of kids so Ste. Vierge will grow and grow."

So that's what they did.

He picks up a twelve-pack of beer.

Manon—Sarah—Christine—Pierrot—Marcel—Nathalie—Louise—Michelle—Hugo—Phillipe—Yvonne—Jeanne . . . that's my mom.

He sets the twelve-pack DSC at the meeting point of the two lines of bottles.

Twelve. Twelve. Twelve.

Throughout the following he sets up a model of the town made of beer boxes covered with papier mâché.

So you see, when I was little there was a lot of people in Ste. Vierge. Well not a lot there, like in Welby. But there was enough kids for a fucking school. Most of them, they were my cousins. But some of them, they weren't. And I'll tell you something. A long time ago there, before I was born, when memère was a kid . . . Ste. Vierge used to be a big place. There was even somewhere to buy grocery. And never mind that, there was even a café. That's fucking true. A café in Ste. Vierge. Ayoi! You don't have to go all the way to town to get a hamburger deluxe.

The story of how Ste. Vierge got his name.

He assumes the role of Père Champagne and does the following in a mock Gregorian chant.

Je suis Père Champagne.

He rings a hand bell as if performing a mass.

Je suis Père Champagne.

He rings the bell again.

Notre Père qui est aux cieux.

He makes the sign of the cross.

    Capri. Caproo. Capri. Caproo.

He rings the bell again.

    Je suis Père Champagne and I come from France.

He rings the bell again.

    France.

He rings the bell again.

    France.

He rings the bell again.

    A long time ago when I was so small the Ste. Vierge, she came to me.

He sings, assuming the voice of the Ste. Vierge as he reveals an eighteen inch tall rubber model of the Ste. Vierge which, for the moment, remains covered with a white veil.

    "Ave Maria."

He resumes the Gregorian chant.

    She came to me in a pile of rocks, and I fall down on my knee.

He kneels and begins to pray fervently to the Ste. Vierge.

    Je vous salut Marie pleine de grâce.

He resumes the Gregorian chant.

    And the Ste. Vierge, she tell me,

In the voice of the Ste. Vierge.

    "Get up. Get up and go. Go far away to Canada."

He resumes the Gregorian chant.

So off I go, go, go. And I travel far, far, far. 'Cause I don't have a car.

He breaks into dance.

And the winter is cold. And the mosquito they bite. And I don't got a place to sleep at night.

He resumes the Gregorian chant.

And when I get here to this pile of rock the Ste. Vierge she come back to me.

In the voice of the Ste. Vierge:

"Ave Mari—"

"Build. Build your church here and the people will come."

He resumes the Gregorian chant.

So I build and build all by myself a church so high with the cross to the sky. And I call this place . . . Ste. Vierge.

He places the Ste. Vierge DSL and removes the white veil.

It was my memère told me that. That's why I know it's true.

The story of Welby.

Once there was a stupid English man, and he had a skinny wife, and his name was Mr. and Mrs. Welby. And one day Mr. Welby he said to his wife, "My dear lady, why don't we go for a ride across the West in our nice horse and buggy?"

He picks up a rusted bedpan.

"Oh yes, let's do it!" So off they go riding across the prairie in their nice horse and buggy.

"Giddy up."

He mounts the bedpan as if it were a saddle and rides across the stage. There is a sound of farting. He stops.

"Mrs. Welby. Was that you?"

"No. It must have been a goose."

"Must have been. Giddy up."

He sets off again. Prolonged farting. He stops again.

"Mrs. Welby. I think we should stop and have some tea."

"I think so too."

And so they stop and they drink their tea—

He drinks from the bedpan.

and they eat their cookie—

He eats from the bedpan.

just like the Queen. And when they're finished they ride off again.

He rides off one more time.

But then they hit a stone. And the wheel, it fall off.

"Oh my star! Oh my goodness! What ever will we do?"

"My good gosh! I don't really know about it. I guess we'll have to live here."

And so they build a town and they call it Welby.

He places the bedpan DSR to indicate the town of Welby.

And that my good friend is not a lie. That my friend is the stupid fucking truth.

During the following he pours gravel from a coal bucket to form a line of gravel from DSR to DSL, connecting Welby to Ste. Vierge.

Hey! Do you know why they call me a bastard? I'll tell you why. It's simple. They call me that because I don't have a dad. I know you think everybody have one and I guess me too I have one but I don't know who he is. I know my dad, he's not French. I know my dad is from town. I know my dad, he fuck my mom and make her pregnant and nobody supposed to talk about that. Everybody supposed to shut up and not talk about that. But still, I hear some things.

He sets down the coal bucket and walks along the gravel road towards Welby.

After they build the road from Welby, everybody in Ste. Vierge, they buy the car. They build the road, the people, they want the car. They need to drive their car to town because it's so fancy here. They have their car, they need to drive their car to town. They need to shop in town. They can't shop in Ste. Vierge. No. They can't get the fancy things they want in Ste. Vierge. They need to shop in town. The IGA! Ooh! The CO-OP! Oohh! The Macleod's! Ooohh! Nobody want to shop at home so it all close down. The grocery store, it close down. The café, it close down. Everything. Kaput!

He makes the sound of a car passing by.

Now this road here, if you keep going that way there, you can get to the highway that take you to the States. A lot of guys from Welby they drive through here because it's a short cut to Minot, North Dakota. You know. They can get their beer and their smoke there because it's cheaper.

He makes the sound of another car passing by.

If you walk in the ditch you can find a lot of beer bottles. Me, I don't like the mess, so I always pick them up. When I have enough I walk to town and I get the money. Usually, I have enough for a hamburger deluxe and a coke at the Chinaman's.

He starts to laugh.

When I was small 'tit Loup, that fucking Métis, he like to play a joke. At night we hide in the ditch and when the cars go by we throw mud and rocks at their windows.

He picks up a rock from the gravel road. He makes the sound of a car approaching. He throws the rock. The car screeches to a halt. He assumes the role of the driver.

"Jesus Christ! What the fuck was that?"

Me and 'tit Loup, we try so hard not to laugh. We hide in the long grass. They can never find us.

He lies back in the ditch.

I like to lie in the ditch at night and look at those stars. Do you know the dipper? The big one? Me, I can find that easy. But I'll tell you something. To me, that's not really such a dipper. To me, that's really an elephant. Well, fuck! You just have to look and see. The box, there, that's the head. And that like that there, that's the trunk. That's not so hard.

Hey! You know an elephant? That's a big guy, eh? Everybody think if you're a big guy, you make a lot of noise, you bump into things, you make a big mess. But that's not true. The elephant, him, in the bush he walk so-o-o quiet. Ssshht!

During the following he does an elephant walk, stepping between the bottles, beginning DSL and arriving DSC.

He move his leg like this . . . so careful . . . and his foot . . . his big round foot there . . . it goes down so soft . . . like this here . . . it doesn't make a noise . . . it doesn't break a branch. And do you know how he does it? If you took his foot there, and you saw inside that big thing you would see little toes pointing like this, like a ballet dancer. And those toes, they don't get sore because the boot he's wearing is like a big pillow. You didn't know about that? A big big guy like him? Walking in the bush tip toe. Really, really quiet.

He notices the twelve-pack.

Ssshhht. You can hear some things when you pretend not to listen.

He goes to sit US of the twelve-pack. He adds a roof to the top of the box, lifts it up and sets it on his knee.

I heard a secret. I heard that when I was born in the back room of memère's big house, there was no doctor, just memère and my mom. It was such a secret not even the priest knew about it. He was very surprise when my memère ask him to baptise a bébé with no mother and no father. Maybe she told him she found me in the garden.

But nobody ever told me nothing. I walk into the room— Sshht! Écoute!

But still, if you listen you can hear some things they say and then you pretend you don't listen and they don't know.

I know that not long after I'm born my mom, she move away and me, I live in the house with my memère and pepère.

I know that no one can never, never, never say "Jeanne," the name of my mom, when my memère is in the room.

I know that some of them—some of my tantes—they don't like me here. Ma Tante Yvonne, she say, "That's too much for maman and papa. They had twelve of us to raise, they don't need another one. Who does she think she is to leave her little bastard, her mess with the maudit anglais. Sshht!"

Maybe they don't talk about it. Maybe they don't want you in their house because they think you're a big fucking mess. But still, you can hear a lot of shit when you pretend you don't listen.

He begins to hum "En passant de la rosier."

Memère's house, it was the biggest in all Ste. Vierge. Chaline! It was big because they had twelve kids. They needed the room, that's all.

He mimes playing the violin.

Pepère him he like to dance. But in Ste. Vierge there was no place to dance. So he would invite all the people in the living room of memère's big house. And I remember he would move all the furniture and we would have a dance.

He sings and dances.

"En passant de la rosier,
J'ai rencontré mon 'tit cavalier.
Il voulait m'embrassé.
J'ai dit 'cout mon 'tit 'fronté."

The Métis them, they could play all the instrument and they could sing really loud. Memère her, she didn't like too much drinking. And the Métis—well, she always used to say, "The Métis, that's good people. But I don't want them in my house." And my pepère, he would tell her, "Never mind Marthe! Swing

ta bottine au fond du boîte à bois!" And he would pick her up
and swing her around and make her scream and laugh.

"En passant de la rosier,
J'ai rencontré mon 'tit cavalier.
Il voulait m'embrassé.
J'ai dit 'cout mon 'tit 'fronté."

Me, maybe I'm only this big, but I remember these dance and
I can hear these song like it was today.

He puts on the elephant nose.

Do you know when an elephant finds the bones of one of
his dead friends he like to pick them up and touch them.
Sometimes he pick them up and put them together like a big
puzzle.

*He removes the nose and begins setting out six cotton flour sacks, a galva-
nized steel bucket, and a paper bag across the US plane of the stage.*

Memère always say, "There's no time to cry. There's no time to
act sad. If you act sad you're just being lazy. Il faut être fort. Il
faut travailler fort. Lave les vaiselles. Lave le plancher. Travaille.
Travaille. Travaille."

One time, me and 'tit Loup we were walking in the bush and
we found a dead horse. And it stink so much and it had bugs
crawling in his mouth. Fuck it stink. And 'tit Loup, him, he
don't like that too much and he puke in the grass and he have
to go home. But me I came back there almost every day. And
I watch the dead horse shrink and shrink until there was just
bones.

You know sometimes when a car drives by it might hit a skunk
or a gopher, or maybe even a fox. I don't like to leave these dead
guys on the road, so when I find them I like to pick them up
and carry them behind the shed so they can rot in peace. When
they finish, and they're just bones, I like to wash them in hot
water. Do you know what I found last night? I found a porcupique! You have to be careful when you carry a porcupique.
Because pique, pique, pique. Ça fait mal, eh? But me, I know
how to carry it so I don't get pique. He's a big guy. I bet you he's
got a lot of bones.

He starts to laugh.

One time that crazy 'tit Loup, he get an idea. He take the scarecrow from memère's jardin and he put that on the road like somebody dead, like this. And we tie a rope around his head and we hide in the ditch. And when the cars come by . . .

A car approaches, screeches to a halt. He assumes the role of the driver.

"Fuck! Somebody's dead on the fucking road."

And just when they come out there, to check about this, me and 'tit Loup we pull the rope, and the scarecrow he jump, and we scare the shit out of them. That 'tit Loup he sure make a good joke.

Do you know about le Vieux Cackoo and Mon Oncle Eli? A lot of people say, "Those two were fucking crazy." But me, I don't think that's so nice to say. I don't think they were so bad.

Mon Oncle Eli him, he was memère's brother and he lived in a shack in the valley with le Vieux Cackoo. When I'm little I used to walk to visit with them. Mon Oncle Eli him, he was always so excited to see me. He would dance in the kitchen. "Ah, seigneur! La grande visite de Ste. Vierge. Il faut faire un beau gâteau. Angel food pour le petit Chou-gras."

Le Vieux Cackoo was deaf and he couldn't talk. And he always want me to play the big piano. Me, I can't play so I just bang like crazy. And him, he would put his ear against the wood and tap his hand and sing, "Guh guh guh guh guh." Mon Oncle Eli would come in laughing, "Quelle belle musique! Chante les boys! Chante fort!"

Then, when the cake was done, we would take it outside with a blanket and have a picnic in the long grass. Mon Oncle Eli him, he would always tell some funny, funny stories. But when he drank more chokecherry wine the stories would be sad and he would start to cry. Sometimes he would cry so much Le Vieux Cackoo would have to hold him and rub his head like a baby until he'd fall asleep. Then we would carry him in the house, and put him in the bed.

When le Vieux Cackoo died mon Oncle Eli him, he was so sad.

In the graveyard he fell in the snow and he yelled, "J'ai perdu mon Cackoo. Je veux mourir." Me, I don't know what to do so I rub his head like this, and I say, "Pleure pas mon Oncle Eli. Il faut être fort. Il faut être fort."

He sings.

There's a house on a hill,
By the worn out, weathered old mill,
In the valley below,
Where the river wind,
There's no such thing as bad times.
In the South, southern plain,
And Cotton Ginny's her name,
And she pick my bum . . .

He takes a bottle of beer from the paper bag and drinks throughout the following.

Labatt's Blue!

Me, I like the night. I like the night because the moon him, he's français. That's right. French. He's round and fat and he always smile and he always tell a good joke. Just like my pepère. And when he drink a bit he sings a good song.

He sings.

"There's a house on the hill."

Eh? That's the Moon. Un vrai bonhomme.

The school in Ste. Vierge, I go there when I'm little. The stupid teacher she make me sit beside Sisco Belhumeur. And he smell like smoke and he always scratch his head, and pick his nose. The teacher, she's Madam Labousse and she can talk French but she tell us we can't talk French in school because, "Now we learn the English." All the older ones, they know how to talk in English and they always laugh at me and Sisco. Sisco he can't talk English, just Cree and French. And me, I know a bit of English, not too much, but I'm too shy to talk. I don't like school. I don't like Madame Labousse. I never understand what she talk about and she always yell at me when I look out the window.

Pepère him, he don't like school. Whenever I don't want to go, he says, "Mais, reste chez nous. Today you help me with the cows."

I don't like the day. I don't like the bright day. And I'll tell you something. You might think I'm some kind of crazy guy but I'll tell you something I know is true. The sun? The sun up there in the sky? She's anglaise. That's right, English. She just sits up and she's so smart and so serious and she can't laugh and she can't tell a joke! She just point at you and she don't smile.

When I was in grade three they built a new school in Welby. A skinny man came from Regina to tell us the Ste. Vierge school would close down. At first I was so happy because I thought, "Fuck! We don't have to go to school." But the skinny man told us there would be a bus to take us to Welby and pepère him, he was the bus driver.

Mrs. Fruin, she was a mean bitch. Every morning, when the Ste. Vierge bus come to school, she would stand in the door and say, "Take off your boot. Take off your boot. You don't want to mess the new school." One day I don't want to take off my boot because I have a hole in my sock and I don't want the kids to tease me.

"You take off those dirty, muddy boots young boy, or I'll pull your ear right off."

"That's not mud on my boot. That's shit. I must have stepped in some cow shit."

Ayoi! Clack across the face and she pull my ear all the way to the office.

"Maybe they talk like pigs where you come from young man, but now you're in Welby and in Welby we don't use dirty words."

On the way back home I told pepère, "The teacher, she slapped my face because I said, 'Shit!' Did you know, shit's a dirty word you? But pepère, he just laugh, and he tell me, "Mrs. Fruin her, she thinks that shit's a dirty word because her, she doesn't shit. She doesn't even have a hole. That's why her ass is so big, because the shit can't come out. That's why she wears so much perfume. To cover the smell of shit." Bien! That's true. My pepère told me it was.

During the following he tips the twelve-pack on its side, takes the beer bottles out, and begins to set them in a circle around him.

Do you know why elephants can't fly anymore? I'll tell you. One time, there was a big fancy teacher, sitting under a tree, teaching a big fancy lesson to all of her kids, "Two plus two. Two plus two." And the elephants, they were floating in the clouds, holding their breath. Well, they need to have a rest. So they stop in the tree. Bien. Well the tree it can't hold so many heavy guys so it breaks and it falls on top of the teacher. Well the teacher her, she was so mad she swore at the elephants and she said a big magic thing there, so bad they forget how to fly. That's true. They forget. After that, they don't fly again.

He begins humming a Christmas carol ("Il est né le divine enfant"), as he puts candles in each of the bottles.

Before Christmas, me and memère, fuck, we were so busy. We have to clean the house. We have to change all the sheet in the bed. We have to make tortière, sucre en crème, pâté de foie. We have to work and work. Because, this year, everybody is coming home for Noël.

He lights the candles and resumes singing "Il est né le divine enfant." He forgets the words and bursts into a chorus of "Angels We Have Heard on High."

And the presents, too, we have to make. Everybody gets something from memère. Something made from papier mâché. That's a lot of work. Sometimes we stay up all night to make sure it's ready.

All the candles are now lit. He blows out the match.

Then, they all show up. The whole family. All my uncles, my aunts, my cousins. The house is full. We hardly have enough place to sleep. Me, I have to put a pillow and blanket under the stairs because my bed is full.

Hey, turn down the lights!

At night, we all go to la messe de minuit. The church is full. There's candles everywhere. The crèche that memère make is up front. And everybody, they get so quiet when Maurice Blouin sing, "Minuit Chrètien c'est l'heure solennel."

Après la messe we all go back to memère's house for le réveillon and we stay up all night. The ladies in the kitchen they make a lunch. The men in the living room they drink Labatt's Blue. And when they get so drunk there, pepère, he puts on Don Messer and we dance and we dance and we don't go to sleep. But always in the morning memère comes in with a big box full of stuff we made for all the other kids. And my cousins, they're so excited about all that stuff. Little horses and cows. Like this here. Ducks. Some sheep. Stuff like that . . .

Pause.

Aahhhh! That's a long time ago. Now everybody move away. Christmas time nobody come around here.

During the following he blows out all of the candles except one.

"It's not right. She can't raise a boy all by herself. We have to send him away. That bitch Jeanne should come and take him. Maman doesn't need her little bastard."

"Je vous salut Marie pleine de grâce . . ."

He forgets the words to "Hail Mary."

"Notre père qui est aux cieux que ton nom sois sanctifier . . ."

He forgets the words to The Lord's Prayer.

Stupid! Stupid! Stupid! Everybody dies. Everybody moves away. You don't have to get fucking crazy about that.

He puts on the elephant nose.

You know a long time before? Before the big ice went all over? It's true the elephant used to look just like a gopher. That's no lie. Just like a gopher. But after the big ice he start to grow and grow. And now the elephant is a big guy and everybody want to kill the elephant. I think he should've stayed the way he was. I think it's better to be a fucking gopher.

He removes the elephant nose.

Pepère died in the kitchen. Before we went to school. He told me to tie his boot. So I did. Then I hear him go:

He makes a grotesque sucking noise.

And I think he's making a joke, so I laugh. But then he fall off
the chair. On the floor. Moving crazy. All blue. Then he stop.

Memère said we had a lot of work to do. We have to clean the
church. We have to clean the house. We have to change all the
sheet in the bed. We have to make tortière, sucre en crème, pâté
de foie. We have to work and work. Because everybody is coming home.

I told memère, "I'm going to miss pepère."

She told me, "Pleure pas Chou-gras. Il faut être fort. Ton pepère
est aux cieux. Aux cieux avec les anges."

He blows out the final candle. The following is spoken in darkness.

One time, at Christmas, after everybody get the present,
memère tell me to go outside by the shed to get some wood
because the fire is almost out. So I dress up there and I go
behind the shed and, fuck! I can't believe it. In front of me, all
over in the fucking snow, is all kind of little animals, just like
the ones we made my cousins . . . only bigger. Des vaches. Des
chevals. Des muttons. Des couchons. And in the snow, painted
red it say, "Joyeux Noël, Chou-gras!" And I can't believe it. I
can't fucking believe it. How did she make all these? When did
she have time to make all of these? And I look back to the house,
and in the window behind the frost I see memère and pepère.
Standing there. Just watching.

O.K. Turn on the lights.

*He removes all the candles from the beer bottles and begins to return the
bottles to their box.*

Now everybody, they move away. Christmas time nobody come
around here. So, I guess I don't have to clean up. Sometimes,
ma Tante Yvonne, that lives in Welby you know, she ask me to
come for Christmas. So, I bring some sucre en crème. That's
easy to make. And her boy there—I don't know his name,
Daryl, Darcy—I can't remember. But the little one, you know.
Anyway, he says he don't want to sit beside me. He says I stink
too much. Yvonne her, she tells him to go eat in the room with

the TV. After supper we all go watch the TV and me I try so hard not to fall asleep. I just want to come home but Yvonne say I sleep in the basement beside the furnace. She make a bed for me.

He finishes placing the last bottle of beer in the box and tips it back up into an upright position.

I don't like town. I don't like the people in town. Pepère always said, "Maudits anglais manqués! They can have the fucking Maple Leafs and they can keep Joe Clark!" And when he was really drunk he would stand in the middle of the room and yell, "God fuck the Queen!"

He begins to laugh. He reaches into his pocket, lifts his hand to his mouth, and covers it with his other hand so the audience cannot see what he is doing. When he finishes, he reveals his mouth which is covered in bright red lipstick. He kisses the air.

One time, me and 'tit Loup, we were picking chokecherries in the bluff across from the church. And that crazy Métis, he make his lips all purple with the juice and he says, "Look at at me I'm a girl. I'm a girl. Kiss me Chou-gras. I'm a horny, horny girl." That 'tit Loup, he sure make me laugh.

Heh? If you come to Ste. Vierge and you want to see inside the church you have to ask me 'cause I got the key. It's really dirty right now. I don't clean that for a long time. Some birds, you know, get in there and they make a big fucking mess. The statue of la Vierge is still there but she's got bird shit piled up on her head. Like a big hat.

He picks up la Vierge.

Hello. Would you like some of this?

He puts lipstick on la Vierge.

One time, me and 'tit Loup we sneak in the church with some choke-cherries and we squeeze the juice on the white face of la Vierge. And you know what she look like? She look like a hooker! When memère saw that she say, "Oh, Seigneur! Qui est-ce qu'a mis de la jam sur la face de la Vierge?" I tell her it was 'tit Loup. "Maudit Métis!" And she lick a Kleenex and she wipe it off and we say the rosary five times.

He wipes the lipstick from his own face and from the statue of la Vierge.

It was the bishop who came all the way from Regina to tell us they were building a new church in Welby and the Ste. Vierge church would close down. "Not enough people live around here." Memère her, she wasn't too happy. When everyone else was going up to kiss his ring, we went home. "Maudit anglais. Jamais. Jamais. Jamais." She said, "We won't go to the church in Welby. We'll go to the church in St. Joseph instead. There the priest is still French and we have a lot of cousins there." But you know, memère her, she can't drive, and me, I'm too small. So memère says, "We can walk. Ce n'est pas trops loin. Maybe ten, twelve miles if we cut through the bush." But, you know, I think it's farther than that, because, fuck, my leg get sore after we walk all day. So sore I don't even listen to the priest in St. Joseph. I just rub my legs. On the way back home we always sit in the long grass and we eat our sandwich. And memère her, she would tell me all kinds of story about when she was a kid. She would always tell me, "Don't forget how to talk French and always remember tes prières."

Talking to her in the sky.

But you know memère, sometimes I forget some things. You can't help that. I've got no one to talk to anymore. They all move away. In the bush there's still some old Métis live there. Chechess. La Veuve. Blondeau. But I don't see them too much.

Yelling really loudly.

Memère! Écoute! Je veux parler français!

Pause.

But I forget a lot.

Speaking to the audience.

Heh! Don't look at me like I'm some kind of crazy guy, okay? Maybe she can't hear me. But maybe she can. So fuck off!

He leaves the stage but after a brief pause returns.

Sorry.

During the following he gets the steel bucket, which is filled with water, adds flour and begins to stir the mixture.

Do you know how to make the glue for papier mâché? You don't? I can't believe it because it's so fucking easy. All you do is take some water. Then you put some flour inside and you mix it up quick so it's not too lumpy. That's all you do. That's easy eh?

He continues to stir the mixture.

After pepère died, memère said we have to keep busy. She said, "J'en ai des idées là." She said she want to make un 'tit parc by the road—"Un zoo là"—full of animals. Animals made from papier mâché. First, we make un veau—a calf, about this big here. Then we make a small pig. Then, because we found some horns in the bush, we make a deer. After that memère, she found in a closet an old fur coat. So we make a bear. He stand up like this and he hold a Labatt's Blue. In his mouth he's got teeth just like a man. We found those under the bed. They were pepère's. We make everything. Even a buffalo. When we were finished with the animals we made a bunch of lemons and we tied them in the trees.

He climbs up behind the SL box.

You know one time, a car driving by there, it stop. And I heard the man say, "Isn't that strange. Hey kid! Who made the art?"

And I tell him, "Don't be stupid! That's not art. That's a zoo. My grandma made that. And me, I help her."

"What's it for?"

"Mind your business. That's what it's for."

And he drive away.

He pours the glue into the box and returns to the stage.

When 'tit Loup move to Ste. Vierge they drove up in an old

truck that made a big bang. 'Tit Loup him, he was sitting in the back there, on top of a bunch of junk, smoking a cigarette and drinking coke. I watch them from the ditch. They were moving their stuff into the Ste. Vierge school. There was his dad, Cinq Sous, and his two sisters, Jig–Jig and Louise. When 'tit Loup saw me in the ditch he walk up to me with a cigarette.

"Hey, funny face. Do you want a smoke?"

"No. Me, I don't smoke. How come you move into the old school?"

"I don't know. My dad bought that."

"Me, I live in that big house with my memère. Do you want to see my zoo?"

When 'tit Loup saw the zoo he ran around like a crazy Métis and he jumped up on the back of the deer. He just laugh and laugh.

During the following he rips a pile of paper and puts it into a small box.

One time, me and memère, we were walking home from St. Joseph. And we were almost home because we were on the gravel road and we could see the church. Well, fuck! A big grey storm started to come to us. And everything got real cold and fucking windy. And we could see like a—a grey thing there, you know . . . uh . . . Christ! What do you call that? Like a tunnel spinning? Fuck! What is that? Well, you know what I mean! Fuck! A grey thing coming straight down the gravel road. Memère her, she grab my hand and we run in the ditch and we crawl in the culvert under the road and we start to pray. "Je vous salut Marie. Je vous salut Marie. Je vous salut Marie." And we don't stop until everything is real quiet. Then, we crawl out of the culvert and we watch the storm move away. And that's when memère get her idea. That's when she said, "Chou-gras, le zoo n'est pas fini!"

You know there is two kinds of elephant? That's right. Two kinds. One is from Africa. And the other one is Chinese. The one from Africa is tall, tall, tall and very skinny. He has big big ears and his back, it scoop down like this. The elephant that memère made for the zoo is Chinese. The Chinese one is round and fat and not so tall and his ears are not so big. I know because I read that in a book and I told memère, "If we're going to make an elephant we have to know which kind to make." And she point to the Chinese one and she say, "Celui-là."

He climbs up behind the SR box.

If you want to make an elephant you have to work hard, because it takes a long time. You can't make an elephant in two fucking days. So don't tell me, "I can make an elephant easy," because that's a fucking lie! I should know. I help memère to make one.

He dumps the ripped paper into the SL box and comes back onto the stage.

First, you have to find the right legs. Me and memère we walk in the bush for a day and when she squint her eye and see the perfect tree, "En aille, coup les."

Then you have to find something good for the body. Us, we use an old bureau from upstairs. Nice and strong and just the right size. We put that on the legs.

For the head we found an old coke box made from wood. Not quite big enough but memère said we could add some pieces. For the ears we use an old tire tube. For the trunk, we took the wood from an old mirror that look like this:

He demonstrates.

We put that together and fuck, that's a trunk.

So when you have all the skeleton you have to hammer and tie that good and tight so the elephant can stand up all by himself.

So there you are. You have an elephant with no skin. Now my friend the fucking work begin. Bring the water, make the glue, find all the paper you have in the house: magazine; the *Welby Spectator*; Christmas paper; everything you can fucking find because the elephant has to be big and fat, just like the picture.

Me, my job is to put the glue nice on the paper and give that to memère so she can put that in the right place. Glue on the paper, give that to memère. Glue on the paper, give that to memère. Glue on the paper—stop! Memère has to check the picture to see, like this:

Assuming the role of his mémère, he uses his thumb to compare the proportions of the elephant in the photo with the elephant they are building.

OK. Glue on the paper, give that to mémère. Glue on the paper, give that to mémère. Glue on the paper, give that to mémère. Glue on the paper . . . holy fuck! There he is. And you can't believe it. You can't believe this big fucking guy.

He stands up and moves around to stand face to face with the elephant.

She took some stones for the eyes and she painted them so real that he stare at you so sad, almost like crying. So sad because here he is. In Ste. Vierge. And maybe he's a million miles from China. I wrap my arm around his big neck and I rub his head and I say in his rubber ear, "Pleure pas. Il faut être fort. Il faut être fort."

It was 'tit Loup's idea to put the wheels on the legs. He said it would be good if one could sit on top and the other one could pull. So that's what we do. We pull our sad elephant all over Ste. Vierge. I told 'tit Loup the elephant was ours, even though mémère said it was just for me.

One time me and 'tit Loup we had a big fucking fight. We were out in the pasture with the elephant eating our sandwich on the hay rack. And 'tit Loup him, he get a crazy idea. He want to teach me how to dance.

"I already know how to dance."

"Not like a Métis, you can't. You can't jig like a half breed." And he get up there and he start doing a funny step on the rack.

"Come on Chou-gras show me how you dance." So me, I get up there and I show him my dance. And 'tit Loup him, he start laughing at me. Laughing and laughing like a crazy Métis.

"Stop laughing, 'tit Loup. It's not so funny."

"I can't help it. You dance like an anglais. You dance like someone from Welby."

"Fuck you, 'tit Loup, you dirty Métis! And quit laughing."

"Fuck you, Chou-gras! You maudit anglais!"

"'Tit Loup, you're nothing but a stupid Métis! And your dad is always drunk!" And I take the rope on the elephant and I start to pull him home.

"And another thing 'tit Loup. The elephant is mine. My memère made it for me. So you can't ride it because she doesn't want no Métis to even touch it."

That's when 'tit Loup, he throw a rock. Capow! Right in the head. And I fall down in the tall grass. The next thing I know 'tit Loup is on top of me. "Wake up, Chou-gras. I'm sorry. Wake up." And he pick me up, and he put me on the elephant, and he pull me all the way home.

I told memère I tripped and fell on a rock and she wiped the blood off my head with a cold cloth.

Memère her, she been to a lot of place. After pepère died she used to go away for visits. Usually she go away to visit my aunts and my uncles that live far away. Me, I have to stay home to make sure everything is alright. One time, memère, she even went to Edmonton to visit ma Tante Louise. She took the train from Welby all the way to Edmonton. And you know what? You won't fucking believe it. When she was in Edmonton she went to a real zoo and she took a ride on a real elephant. That's pretty good eh? Memère on a real elephant. They even took a picture. She said the skin was rough, rough, rough, but she said the trunk at the bottom there was soft to touch. Soft like a little baby's hand.

A long painful pause.

The first time I'm drunk is with 'tit Loup. Memère was gone to visit in Regina, and me, I was supposed to keep care of the house. 'Tit Loup said, "Hey! Let's have a party. We'll tell some guys in Welby and we'll have a party in the big house." Me, I'm nervous. I don't want a fucking party. But 'tit Loup say, "Come on Chou-gras. Don't be an old lady. Let's have some fun. It's so boring in Ste. Vierge."

When the bar in Welby closes they all show up. Eight Ball. Bobby Welcher. Minty. That stupid Murray Lloyd. All the gang. All the ones that never talk to me but when there's a party they all show up with their case of fucking Molson beer and they act like your best fucking friend.

Me, you know, I'm so nervous. I drink a lot and I drink fast. I'm nervous because I don't want these maudits anglais to wreck the house. I heard there was a fight outside and I don't want that in the house.

Bobby Welcher him, he's in the middle of the room stomping his foot so hard. All the windows are shaking. The girls are drunk and they're laughing at him, but he just keeps dancing like a big joke.

'Tit Loup, he tells me, "You're acting so weird, Chou-gras. Don't worry. Everybody is having a good time. Tomorrow we can clean. Go get another beer."

When I go in the kitchen I see that stupid Murray Lloyd. He's got eggs from the fridge and he's breaking them on the floor. Everybody is laughing. It's supposed to be a funny fucking joke.

"Don't do that, Murray. It's not so funny."

And I go to pick up the mess. And Murray, he breaks an egg on my head. And everyone is laughing at me. And I try to get up but I slip on some eggs. I want to find 'tit Loup. I want him to make everybody go away from memère's big house. I don't want this party anymore.

When I find 'tit Loup he's holding some girl. He's got his face pressed against some girl's face . . . and his tongue is all . . . his tongue is all . . . And the room is spinning. And Bobby Welcher is dancing. And the windows are shaking. And I have to run outside. I've got shit in my hair and I'm gonna be sick. And I run down the road. I run and I run like I think I'm going crazy. And when I get to the church I stop, and I look up, and in the window upstairs I see the moon. I see the moon in the window of the Ste. Vierge church. And just before I puke all over the gravel, I yell, "God fuck the Queen!"

That's when I hear a noise. The noise of a car that slam the brakes on the gravel road. And a bang, like it hit something. And I see the lights of a car down by memère's house. And I hear, "What the fuck did we hit?"

Run. Run back to the house. Run to the circle of guys standing on the gravel road.

I see Eight ball. I see Bobby Welcher. I see that stupid Murray Lloyd. "Hey J.C., maybe you should put up a sign on the road: ELEPHANT CROSSING."

And I see my elephant down on the road. In the light of the car that hit him. On the road like this . . . with his side smashed in . . . and his head all twist like this . . . and his sad stone eye falls out on the gravel with red Christmas paper showing through . . . just like blood.

Me, I'm like ice and I can't move. I'm scared to talk because maybe I might cry.

"Who put that guy on the road?"

"Maybe he walk out all by himself."

"Shut up Murray!"

It's 'tit Loup. And I see him there holding hands with the girl he kiss in the house. And I see something in his dirty half breed face. And I start to get hot, so hot. And I know. I remember the scarecrow and I know.

"Maudit fucking Métis!"

And I swing my fist like I never did before and I crack him one in the face. And the girl, she scream when 'tit Loup him, he fall down on the road holding a hand full of blood. And I yell, swinging at all of them, "Everybody go. Everybody go away or I'll kill you. I'll kill you."

Angry at himself for letting the audience see him cry.

There's no time to cry. There's no time to act sad. If you act sad you're just being fucking lazy. When my memère died ten years ago I didn't cry. I didn't cry. I didn't cry. I was too fucking busy. I have to clean the house. I have to change all the sheet in the bed. I have to make tortière, sucre en crème, pâté de foie. I work and work. The church, too, I clean. I scrape the bird shit from the bench. I shake the mice out of the tabernacle. I even wash the big curtain behind the altar.

There's no time to cry. There's no time to act sad. Il faut être fort. Il faut travailler fort. Travail. Travail. Travail.

Pause.

A while ago I go back to the place in the long grass and I find my elephant. There's not much left of him. Just a lot of junk, you know, wood and old paper with grass growing through it. And there I am in the tall grass with the bones of my elephant. And everything is so quiet. And everything doesn't move. And that's when I heard a whisper, so quiet in my ear, almost like a kiss. And it say, "Hey, funny face! You wanna smoke?" And that's when I get my idea. That's when I know what I'm gonna do.

I'm gonna make an elephant. I'm gonna make an elephant so fucking big that when he stand over the gravel road the cars, they can drive right through his legs. I'm gonna make an elephant so fucking big that the people they can see it from Welby. They can see it from St. Joseph. They can see it all the way from Minot fucking North Dakota. And the people, they're gonna come from all over to see this big fucking guy. They're gonna come from all over the world. And Ste. Vierge . . . Ste. Vierge is gonna grow and grow.

He returns to ripping paper. As he does so he sings, "En passant de la rosier."

Slow fade to black.